Text for Scotland

Building Excellence in Language

BOOK 2

Caroline Harper
Gary Smith
Series Editor: Colin Eckford

www.heinemann.co.uk
✓ Free online support
✓ Useful weblinks
✓ 24 hour online ordering

01865 888118

Contents

Contents

1 Communication

Experiences and outcomes

In this unit you will:

Reading
- identify how different texts are organised and laid out, and what effect this creates
- consider how different audiences might respond to texts
- express preferences and opinions about texts
- learn how and why writers use different degrees of formality and informality.

Writing
- plan your writing so that you develop strong arguments
- use paragraphs correctly to sequence your ideas
- write a variety of arguments, both for and against an issue, and from a balanced point of view.

Words and sentences
- use pronouns correctly to write in the third person
- identify examples of colloquial language and suggest more formal alternatives
- use exclamation marks to alter the tone of sentences
- use speech punctuation and apostrophes for possession.

By the end of this unit you will:

- read and answer questions on a variety of articles about space exploration (Reading Activity: Reading for information)
- write a review of a television programme in a balanced style (Writing Activity: Functional writing).

1 Communication forms

You are learning:
- to recognise how different types of communication are organised and understand how ICT has influenced the style of language.

Many new forms of communication have become popular in the twenty-first century. ICT means that we can keep in touch with others more easily, for work and leisure. We need to:
- be aware of the new language and vocabulary associated with these new forms
- understand how to communicate in these different media
- recognise both the advantages and risks of these new forms.

Activity 1

1 How many of the communication forms below are you familiar with?

2 Which of the communication forms below do you think are new and were not available to previous generations – for example, your parents and grandparents – when they were teenagers?

- wiki
- instant messaging/SMS
- radio
- email
- blogs
- websites
- TV advertisements
- newspapers
- social networking sites
- mail
- phone

a Which communication form do you think is the slowest?
b Which communication form is the quickest?
c Identify any terms that you are not familiar with and find out what they mean. You could use the Internet or ask others.
d What advantages do you think these new forms of communication give your generation that were not available to your grandparents?
e What disadvantages do you think there are?

Activity 2

Social networking sites are a popular way of communicating and exchanging information. MySpace is an example of a social networking site, while Facebook defines itself as a 'social utility' that connects users with the people around them. It has been said that these sites have been used to make famous people ordinary and ordinary people famous! The singer Lily Allen launched her career using MySpace.

Look at the text below from Facebook. Look carefully at the organisational features of this page – for example images, links, menus, colour, headings. Write a sentence for each one, explaining why you think it has been used and how effective you think it is.

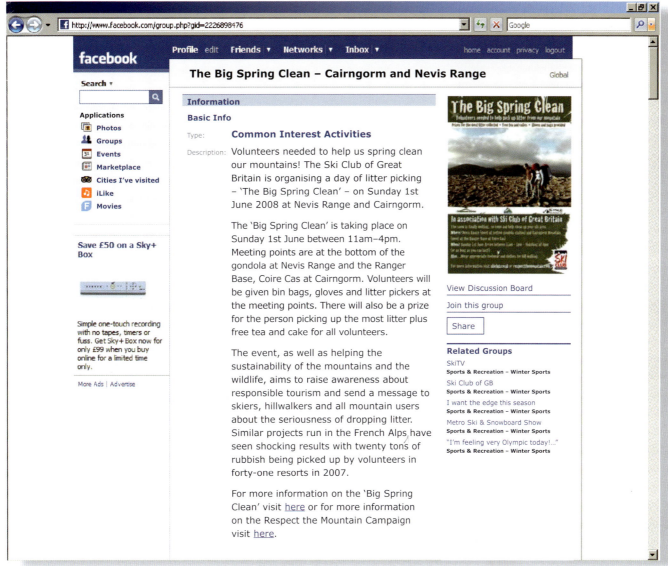

The Big Spring Clean group

Facebook is a registered trademark of Facebook, Inc.

Self-evaluation

You are learning to identify how texts such as social networking pages are organised. Decide which level you are working at and what your target for improvement is.

Beginner	Competent	Expert
I can identify and describe features of layout and presentation.	I can explain the impact that layout and presentation have on an audience.	I can discuss the effectiveness of features of layout and presentation, saying how successful they are.

2 Safety and communication

You are learning:
● to select key points from your reading.

As the Internet has allowed young people to widen their networks of communication, safety issues have become increasingly important.

Activity 1

1　Read the extract below from a website advising young people about Internet safety.

a　What is the difference between the black text and the blue text in this article?

b　What is the purpose of the first paragraph in italics?

c　What potential risks does this webpage highlight for young people who use the Internet? Divide these into two groups of risks:

● Personal safety

● Money and equipment

Summarise these risks in bullet points.

yOUNGsCOT.oRG
SCOTTISH YOUTH INFORMATION FOR 11–26 YEAR OLDS

Web Safety

Now we aren't getting heavy here, just a bit protective – hey, we care! So sue us … We want everyone to be happy and healthy, and for the most part the Internet is a fabulous thing. But, as in all walks of life, it can attract a variety of … let's say unconventional and sometimes downright dubious activity.

Because of that, it makes sense to keep safe out there in the wondrous world of the Internet, just as you would out there in the non-virtual planet. You wouldn't just reveal all your most personal information to a random person on the street now would you? Would you? If you answered yes to this question, get in touch, we've got some Helplines you can call …

Anyway, sneak a peek at the following to keep safe and hassle free …

Always

- Keep your password safe and don't tell anyone else.
- Be careful in chat rooms. Just because it says that it's only for young people, there's no way to tell if only young people are using it. It might be someone trying to trick you.
- Use a nickname instead of your real name in chatrooms, or when chatting with anyone on the Internet in any other way.
- If someone says something that makes you feel uncomfortable or worried, then leave the chat room. Make sure you tell someone, either your mum or dad, or a carer.
- Be yourself and don't pretend to be someone else – no matter how attractive the option of leading a double life! If you aren't 18 yet then steer clear of sites that say they are for over 18s. It's a huge temptation we know, but trust us – the warnings are there to protect you! If nothing else, it could also end up costing you a fortune on your telephone bills.
- Keep any four-letter expletives to yourself – you know what they say, swearing shows a real lack of imagination!
- Don't give out your main (or only) email address. Keep it private. If you want to give out an email address choose a disposable address, e.g. a second Hotmail address.
- Before you leave a computer remember to log out of all the sites you have logged on to. This way nobody can pretend to be you, or use services that only you're entitled to use.

A few other Hints 'n' Tips…

- If you are chatting to people on the Internet, then don't tell anyone you talk to any of your personal details, especially your address, telephone number or school, etc.
- Don't ever send anyone your picture, any of your bank details, or credit card details without first checking with a responsible adult. You can check if a site is secure by looking to the bottom of your screen for a lock/padlock icon. If it is locked then the site is secure. For more info you can click on the padlock.
- Don't sign up for a get rich quick scheme. If it sounds too good to be true then it probably is. If not then it may even end up costing you money.
- Don't arrange to meet anyone unless your parent or carer (or your most responsible friend – you know, the one who saves their money, has got a pension already, that sort of thing) goes with you and you meet in a very public place with lots of people around. As the ads in the cinema suggest the people you contact online are not always who they say they are. No one can check if your 'keypals' are what they claim – because no one can see them.
- Don't open email attachments unless they are from someone you already know and trust. Attachments can contain viruses or other programmes that can destroy all the information and software on your computer. That even includes your latest essay and all the cheaters tips on Championship Manager.
- Don't respond to nasty, suggestive messages, or rude pictures. Tell your parent or carer to report them to your Internet Service Provider immediately.

Activity 2

1 'You wouldn't just reveal all your most personal information to a random person on the street now would you?'

Why has the writer chosen to make this a question rather than a statement?

2 'Don't open email attachments unless they are from somebody you already know and trust.'

Why do you think the writer chose to begin this sentence with 'Don't' rather than 'You shouldn't'? What difference does it make to the tone?

3 'Keep your password safe and don't tell anyone else.'
'Be careful in chat rooms.'

Are these two sentences statements, questions or commands? What effect does the writer achieve as a result?

Activity 3

Copy the table below and complete it using relevant information from the article.

Key advice when using social networking sites	Key advice on protecting your personal details on the Internet	Key advice on personal safety
Be careful about what personal information you share	Check with a responsible adult before sending bank details	Don't respond to nasty, suggestive messages or rude pictures

Activity 4

1 Select what you think are the three most important pieces of advice and use them to write a paragraph for your school website giving advice about Internet use.

2 Which do you think is the single most important piece of advice for your age group? Give reasons for your choice.

Knowledge about language First, second and third person

The first person is used to refer to yourself – for example, 'I am a student.' The second person is used to give advice – for example, 'If **you** are chatting to people on the Internet, then don't tell anyone **you** talk to any of **your** personal details.' The third person is used to refer to someone else – for example, '**He** is in the library.'

Rewrite the passage below in the third person (replacing 'you' with 'young people' or 'they'). What difference does this make to the tone?

You have to be careful when using social networking sites. You have to remember that information uploaded to these sites cannot easily be removed. Later you may regret putting up an embarrassing picture or too honest an account of a party – but by then it may have been copied and used by thousands of others.

3 Privacy and communication

You are learning:
● to recognise how writers organise features of a text.

In some new areas of communication, such as text-messaging and social networking, teenagers have been one of the fastest-growing user groups. Teenagers have been active in creating their own cultures and languages as part of this use.

Activity 1

1 Read the newspaper extract below that reviews a variety of parents' opinions about privacy and communication.

How far would you go?

She's 14, looks 18, and is full of attitude. You want to find out what's going on in her world ... Sophie Radice talks to parents who snoop on their teens' cyber secrets

The Guardian, Saturday October 20, 2007

Victoria, 50, has four daughters aged between nine and 18

'You're not a good parent if you don't know what your kids are doing. In what other part of their life do you just sign off responsibility and leave them to cope on their own? In a casual way, I check their Bebo sites, their mobiles and look in their address books in their mobiles to make sure that everything is OK and that things are not getting out of hand. I am pretty good at teen speak now and I can tell any parent who wants to know.

'My kids are aware that I do a bit of light monitoring and seem pretty used to it by now. I can reassure parents who wouldn't dream of prying that most of what goes on is pretty dull. At first I was really shocked by the photos they put up and then I realised that, particularly on MSN and MySpace, they create wilder, more interesting personas that often bear little relation to who they are and what they are really doing. It's often quite funny and creative and they really listen to each other's music and poetry.'

Jane, 39, has two sons aged six and 15

'I wouldn't have even thought of going through my son's things, until he started staying out without telling me where he was. I had quite a few nights last summer when I rang around hospitals, police stations, and all his friends trying to find him. When he came home he didn't seem to care how scared I was. He still won't tell me where he is and just turns off his phone.

'I'm a single mum and I feel that I have to find new ways to find out what is going on, and so if I can go through his phone when he has put it down or have a look at what he is writing on his MSN then I will. That way I find out where he has been, what he is planning and who he is seeing.'

Richard, 57, has three daughters aged 25, 23 and 19

'My youngest daughter was on my laptop and left her email on the screen, which I happened to see was from my middle daughter, who is at university. She talked a lot about how much she is drinking and about not doing any work and also said something slightly derogatory about my wife, which was a bit unkind, although not serious. I didn't think much of it so said casually to my youngest daughter that I had seen it and that she was lucky to have heard from her. Well, it completely blew up in my face because my youngest daughter said that we had always taught them to respect other people's property and there I was just looking at private stuff and who did I think I was? Some patriarch who thought he had the right to snoop?

'I had my wife and all my daughters completely livid with me. I did try to say that it was just left up there for me to see and that I would have to have had no interest in my daughters whatsoever not to read something that was right in front of me.'

Alex Thomson
was hear

2 List the different opinions that are offered by parents about checking on their teenagers and decide where each parent's name should go on the chart below.

Parents should
not check

Parents should
definitely check

3 a Write a sentence summing up each parent's attitude to checking on their teenagers.
b What do you think about the opinions of each of the parents in the article?
c Select one quotation from each parent that you either agree with or disagree with. Write a comment next to each quotation expressing your point of view.
d How do you think different audiences might respond to this text? For example, adults who have children, adults who don't, teenagers and so on.

Activity 2

Newspapers make choices about presentational features in order to engage their readers. Look at the presentational features of the newspaper article on page 10 (the image, text formatting and colour) and answer the questions below.

1 How might the image catch the interest of the intended reader?

2 How is text formatting such as emboldening and different font sizes used to structure the article and interest the reader in the examples that follow?

Victoria, 50, has four daughters aged between nine and 18

She's 14, looks 18, and is full of attitude.

How far would you go?

Activity 3

Look at the quotations below and comment on how language is used to interest the reader.

'You want to find out what's going on in her world'

'How far would you go?'

'parents who snoop on their teens' cyber secrets'

Activity 4

The articles on pages 8 and 10 both highlight some of the dangers of modern communications for young people.

1   Consider the differences between the style and content of the two articles by copying out the table below and inserting the correct terms from the word bank. An example has been filled in for you.

Feature	*Young Scot* 'web safety' article	*Guardian* 'Family' article
Intended audience		
Purpose	writing to advise	
Language style		
Presentational features	• • •	• • •

Word bank

formal	use of second person
informal	questions to include the reader
colloquial language	bullet points
humour	use of personal accounts

2   Now choose three features from those listed above and write a paragraph contrasting the two texts, using examples to support your points. Explain to what extent each feature makes the text more enjoyable or interesting to read, giving reasons for your opinion.

Knowledge about language Colloquial language

In both the *Young Scot* website extract and the *Guardian* article, colloquial language is used. This includes:

- the use of **contractions** ('wouldn't' rather than 'would not' and 'she's' rather than 'she is')

- the use of **informal slang** terms ('heavy', 'hey', 'teen speak').

1   Find two other slang terms from the *Young Scot* extract and two other slang terms from the *Guardian* article, and write them down.

2   Think of a more formal expression for each slang term you found and write that beside them.

3   Which article has more informal slang terms? Why do you think that is?

Self-evaluation

Look at your responses to Activity 4 on page 12. How confident did you feel comparing the two texts? Use the table below to identify the level of your reading skills.

Beginner	Competent	Expert
• I can identify the audience and purpose of a text • I can make some comments on the presentational and language features in a text	• I can identify and discuss similarities and differences between different types of texts	• I can clearly state the purpose and audience and compare and contrast different texts, explaining why there are these differences and similarities

4 Formal and informal communication

Another popular modern form of communication is the blog. Many social networking pages or personal webpages contain links to blogs. A blog (web log) is a website where entries are written in **chronological order**. Many provide commentary or news on a particular subject; others function as more personal online diaries. A typical blog combines text and images plus links to other blogs, webpages and media related to its topic.

Activity 1

Read the three diary entries (Texts 1–3) that follow, then link each one to its correct author and decide whether it is a blog or a handwritten diary. Give reasons for your choices.

Explanation

chronological order time order; the order in which things happen

(a) Moby (born Richard Melville Hall, 11 September 1965) is an American songwriter, musician and singer, well known for his political and environmental beliefs.

(b) James Boswell (29 October 1740 – 19 May 1795) was a lawyer and the biographer of Samuel Johnson, who wrote one of the first English dictionaries. His diaries describe his life in the eighteenth century and his travels elsewhere in Scotland.

(c) Joan Lennon is a children's novelist. She is the author of fantasy fiction including *The Seventh Tide*, *Questors* and *The Wicket Chronicles*.

Text 1

saturday

on saturday i'm going upstate to an animal sanctuary where, in theory, i'll be able to play with pigs and cows that have been rescued from those happy places where they torture and kill pigs and cows. have i mentioned that i'm a vegan ...? here's my simple request ...
in a perfect world animals would not suffer for human purposes. but we don't live in a perfect world. in a perfect world we'd all be vegans. again, we don't live in a perfect world. i'm not going to be presumptuous and tell you that you should be a vegan or a vegetarian. what i will ask is that you ask yourself the question:
'could i look into an animal's eyes and say: my hunger is more important than your suffering?' let your conscience be your guide. if you do choose to eat meat and/or dairy products could you at least consider eating compassionately farmed meat and/or dairy? ... thanks for listening.

Text 2

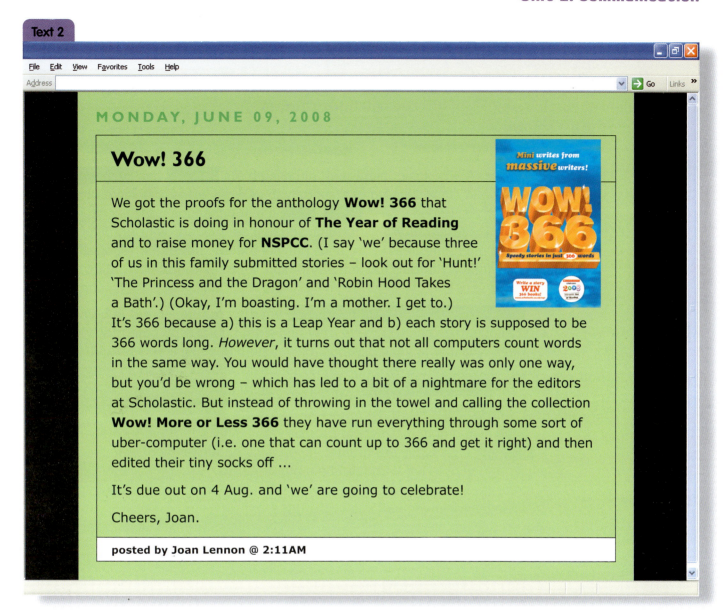

MONDAY, JUNE 09, 2008

Wow! 366

We got the proofs for the anthology **Wow! 366** that Scholastic is doing in honour of **The Year of Reading** and to raise money for **NSPCC**. (I say 'we' because three of us in this family submitted stories – look out for 'Hunt!' 'The Princess and the Dragon' and 'Robin Hood Takes a Bath'.) (Okay, I'm boasting. I'm a mother. I get to.)

It's 366 because a) this is a Leap Year and b) each story is supposed to be 366 words long. *However*, it turns out that not all computers count words in the same way. You would have thought there really was only one way, but you'd be wrong – which has led to a bit of a nightmare for the editors at Scholastic. But instead of throwing in the towel and calling the collection **Wow! More or Less 366** they have run everything through some sort of uber-computer (i.e. one that can count up to 366 and get it right) and then edited their tiny socks off ...

It's due out on 4 Aug. and 'we' are going to celebrate!

Cheers, Joan.

posted by Joan Lennon @ 2:11AM

Text 3

Was too late of getting up, and fretted by being hurried and when my wife joked, was exasperated, threw my tea into the fire, and went out without breakfast. It was a frosty morning. I found that I had supposed it later than it was so went and breakfasted at my father's.

15

Activity 2

Blogs are generally characterised by informal language and informal style.

1   How many different examples of this can you find in Text 1?
    Complete the list below:

> • no capital letters at the beginning of sentences
> • contractions such as *I'm*, *don't*.

2   Find examples of informal style or language in Texts 2 and 3.
    Which text is most formal? Give reasons for your choice.

Activity 3

Like a personal diary, a blog is a place where people can reveal much about their character, thoughts and lifestyle. What do you learn about the character, thoughts and lifestyle of the writer from Text 1? Use examples and quotations to support your points. You might use the sentence starters below to help you.

What we learn	Quotations
We learn about Moby's lifestyle through his comments about food ...	have i mentioned that i'm a vegan ...?
We learn that Moby is not shy about speaking about his political views ...	
We learn that Moby is a sociable musician who is using his blog to talk to his fans ...	

Knowledge about language — Exclamations

Exclamation marks can be used when someone cries out, gives an order, shouts, or says something forcefully or humorously.

Look at this modernised dialogue between James Boswell and his wife, based on the diary account on page 15.

> 'I've slept in. I'm going to be late for work.'
> 'How dreadful – the famous lawyer, James Boswell, late for work. The Scottish justice system will not survive such a calamity.'
> 'How dare you make fun of me? Forget the tea – I'm leaving this minute.'
> 'Oh. You've put the fire out, throwing your tea on it. What a ridiculous thing to do.'

Choose the three best places where you could replace a full stop with an exclamation mark. Then compare your results with a partner's and discuss the reasons for your answers. How do your exclamation marks change the meaning or the tone of these sentences?

Reading Activity

Reading for information

Holidays in space – a good idea or not?

Read texts A–D on pages 17–19, then complete the tasks that follow.

Text A

http://www.logo.com/newsletter/11/holidays.htm

Logotron :: Article – Holidays in Space

Logotron educational software

Partners with the teaching profession – Pioneers in Learning

home / about / products / support / my cart / search

Holidays in space

On May 25, 1961, President Kennedy first voiced a goal, 'before this decade is out, of landing a man on the moon and returning him safely to the earth'. It captured the public imagination. It was like Columbus all over again and you felt you were riding on the crest of a wave of human achievement.

National pride had its part to play, of course. The Space Race was essentially between the two great superpowers, America and Russia, and everyone supported one side or the other as if it were a global football competition.

The culmination, as everybody knows, was Neil Armstrong, who on 21st July 1969 set foot on the moon for the first time ever and uttered those immortal words, 'That's one small step for man but one giant leap for mankind.'

Everybody thought that by the end of the century we'd be taking holidays on the moon – or at the very least on a space station – but somehow this has never happened. After that first momentous landing, enthusiasm for space exploration seemed to slowly fizzle out. True, a few more astronauts walked on the moon, and there is a space shuttle which flies up and down regularly; there's even a half-built space station, but it's nothing like we imagined.

So what changed? Did we become bored with space? Did the shuttle disasters shake our faith in the value-versus-cost of space travel? Or did problems on earth get worse and make us try to sort out hunger and poverty before embarking on such a costly exercise as space exploration?

The answer is actually far more mundane than that and like many things, it all comes down to money.

Space exploration seems to be extortionately expensive. We see it as something quite different from anything that has happened before. The Wright brothers' first flight, for example, seems quite straightforward and inexpensive when compared to colonising the moon. Space travel, by contrast, can only happen if literally billions of dollars are poured into it – and that's something only the taxes of the very richest nations could ever finance.

Or so we think.

In fact, human flight was exactly the same as space flight in that it is a challenge which takes place at the very cutting edge of technology. There is no difference. The Wright brothers didn't need to be funded by a national programme paid by taxes and nor should space. If they had, we might still be waiting for the first package holiday to Spain instead of waiting for the first package holiday to the moon.

The Wright brothers used their own money to fund their experiments and eventually, as we all know, they succeeded at Kittyhawk in 1903. What we don't know is that their modern counterparts are doing exactly the same thing all over the world right now. Inventive and creative people are experimenting with the technology of space flight day in and day out and what's more, they're funding their work through raffles and barbeques!

Occasionally we see one of them in that last amusing spot on the news. They are usually shown as harmless eccentrics and we have a quiet chuckle before the next programme starts. But in reality, they are getting far closer than we think to solving some of the problems of space flight.

One thing that is driving their enthusiasm is the 'X Prize'. You may not have heard of it because it's not widely publicised. The X Prize is 'a $10,000,000 prize to jumpstart the space tourism industry through competition between the most talented entrepreneurs and rocket experts in the world.'

Text B

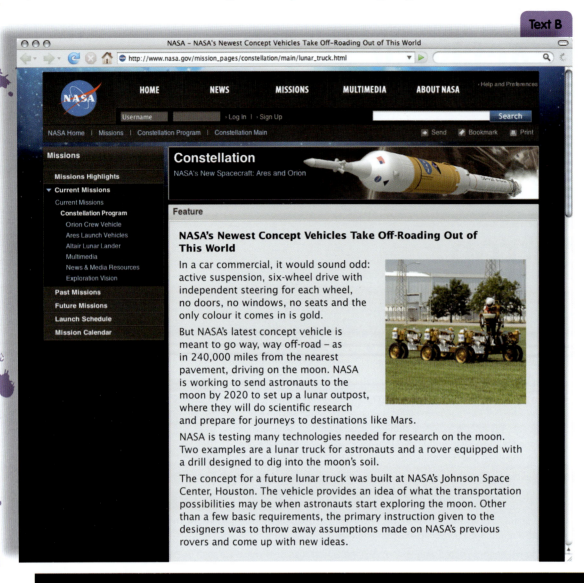

NASA – NASA's Newest Concept Vehicles Take Off-Roading Out of This World

http://www.nasa.gov/mission_pages/constellation/main/lunar_truck.html

HOME NEWS MISSIONS MULTIMEDIA ABOUT NASA · Help and Preferences

Username · Log In | · Sign Up   Search

NASA Home | Missions | Constellation Program | Constellation Main   Send Bookmark Print

Missions

Missions Highlights
▼ Current Missions
Current Missions
Constellation Program
Orion Crew Vehicle
Ares Launch Vehicles
Altair Lunar Lander
Multimedia
News & Media Resources
Exploration Vision
Past Missions
Future Missions
Launch Schedule
Mission Calendar

Constellation
NASA's New Spacecraft: Ares and Orion

Feature

NASA's Newest Concept Vehicles Take Off-Roading Out of This World

In a car commercial, it would sound odd: active suspension, six-wheel drive with independent steering for each wheel, no doors, no windows, no seats and the only colour it comes in is gold.

But NASA's latest concept vehicle is meant to go way, way off-road – as in 240,000 miles from the nearest pavement, driving on the moon. NASA is working to send astronauts to the moon by 2020 to set up a lunar outpost, where they will do scientific research and prepare for journeys to destinations like Mars.

NASA is testing many technologies needed for research on the moon. Two examples are a lunar truck for astronauts and a rover equipped with a drill designed to dig into the moon's soil.

The concept for a future lunar truck was built at NASA's Johnson Space Center, Houston. The vehicle provides an idea of what the transportation possibilities may be when astronauts start exploring the moon. Other than a few basic requirements, the primary instruction given to the designers was to throw away assumptions made on NASA's previous rovers and come up with new ideas.

Text C

Meet an Astronaut!

Are you excited by space travel? Would you love to meet a real astronaut, face-to-face? Well now's your chance! For a limited time only, come to the Kennedy Space Centre Visitor Complex and meet our highly trained and experienced astronauts.

You will have the opportunity to ask your burning questions about space exploration and listen to inspirational stories directly from the people who have lived and worked in space. You will learn about what it takes to become a NASA astronaut and about the amazing discoveries being made in space right now!

The Meet an Astronaut program runs from 5 May until 2 June. Places are limited so book now to avoid disappointment. Booking forms are available via our website.

Text D

File Edit View Favorites Tools Help

Address http://www.postyourcomments.com

Post your comments

Question: Is space travel a good thing, or is it a waste of time and money?

Add your comment

Comments

Space travel provides us with the opportunity to discover new planets, solar systems and maybe one day even new life-forms. It's definitely a good thing!

Ryan, Cardiff

I think the huge amount of money spent on space travel would be far better spent on stamping out child poverty and treating and preventing famine and disease around the world.

Salma, Glasgow

Think of all the new technology that's come about because of space travel and exploration. It's got to be a good thing.

Graham, Dundee

If we continue to explore the universe and uncover its secrets, we may find solutions to the global energy crisis, or even find another place where humans can live.

Pritesh, Birmingham

Pollution and climate change are huge issues on planet earth; sending shuttles into space is only making matters worse.

Alison, Inverness

There are vast areas of this planet which we still know very little about – for example, the oceans and rainforests. Shouldn't we be concentrating on exploring and protecting them before we spend even more money on space travel?

Pat, Kent

Your task

1 Pick out the key events given in the first four paragraphs of Text A and list them in chronological order.

2 The writer makes comparisons between events in the past and events related to space travel.

   a Complete the table below, identifying two pairs of events that are linked. One has been done for you:

Event 1	Event 2
Columbus discovering America	Neil Armstrong landing on the Moon

   b Why do you think the writer has done this?

3 Imagine you had to give a brief radio report based on the key ideas in this article.

   a List the key ideas.

   b Write them up into a report to be read on the radio.

4 What does the phrase 'a global football competition' suggest about the space race?

5 What does the sentence 'enthusiasm for space exploration seemed to slowly fizzle out' suggest about people's view of space travel?

6 Re-read paragraph 5. What effect do you think the writer wanted to achieve by asking this series of questions?

7 What is the effect of printing some words and phrases in a different colour?

8 How does the writer try to make the reader interested in this article? Your answer should include comments on:
   ● the way the writer tries to make the reader feel involved
   ● the choice of language to describe different events
   ● the use of pictures to make the article appealing
   ● any other features that make the article interesting.

Web texts

Text B gives information about holidays in space; Text C tries to persuade you to visit the Kennedy Space Center.

9 Copy and complete the table below, explaining some of the similarities and differences between these two texts.

Feature	Text B: NASA webpage	Text C: Meet an Astronaut!
Similarities in content		
Differences in content		
Similarities in purpose/ effect on the reader		
Differences in purpose/ effect on the reader		
Similarities in choice of style/use of language		
Differences in choice of style/use of language		
Similarities in structure/ presentation		
Differences in structure/ presentation		

10 Identify and list all the arguments **for** space travel and **against** space travel in Text D.

11 Choose two of the comments and write a response to the arguments each one puts forward. You can use ideas and arguments from elsewhere in the material you have been given.

12 Look again at all the texts on pages 17–19.

   a List the main arguments in favour of space travel.

   b List the main arguments against space travel.

   c Write a letter to a newspaper, summarising the arguments **either** for **or** against space travel and adding your own opinions.

5 Subject-specific language

You are learning:
- to plan writing and develop ideas to suit a specific audience.

Earlier in this unit you considered how ICT has influenced and changed language. Other groups in society also have their own vocabularies and forms of language. The review below is about performances by two bands at the T in the Park festival.

Activity 1

1   Read the text opposite and make a list of any subject-specific words or phrases that show this article is a music review.

2   Underline any unfamiliar words or phrases in your list. First, guess their meaning using the context of the article. Then use a dictionary or the Internet to check their definitions.

T in the Park 2006: Main Stage Sunday

With proven big stage performers like Primal Scream, The Charlatans, Kasabian and Feeder all demoted to tents this evening it's hard to see why cockney geezers Hard-Fi are filling such an elevated slot on the Main Stage. And the maths of an extended show and one album to fill it quickly adds up. The hit singles from *Stars of CCTV* in short supply, filler tracks are left to make up the numbers before the stomping drum beat and instantly recognisable riff of The White Stripes' 'Seven Nation Army' can be heard. A massacre takes place as the simple yet awesome piece of music is chewn up and spat back out in a horribly overdone cover. 'Hard To Beat' and 'Cash Machine' prove to be brief highlights.

With Arctic Monkeys, there's no such problems. No big back-drop, no fancy lights and no on-screen imagery; just four English lads with a bag of top modern rock 'n' roll tunes and cheeky grins to a swollen crowd of devotees. From the opening barrage of hypnotic drumming on 'View From The Afternoon' to juke-box goldcard 'I Bet You Look Good On The Dance Floor', everything they do is just right. In stark contrast to Hard-Fi, the tracks from the Monkey's limited catalogue all sound like hits from your childhood, and the crowd is swept away by the music which backs up the incredible hype, which maybe, just maybe, is right for once.

Activity 2

1   As the popularity of the T in the Park festival continues to grow, so does the variety of people who attend the festival. Think about who might be the intended audience(s) of this review and what the purposes of the review might be. Add your ideas to the list below.

Audience	Purpose
People who did not manage to get tickets to the festival	To encourage people's interest in future festivals
Commercial companies involved in the music/record world	

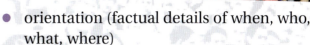

2 Which do you think would be most appropriate for the audiences and purposes you have identified – an informal or formal writing style? Give reasons for your answer.

Activity 3

Look at the features of a review text listed below. Copy out an example from the review on page 22 to illustrate each one. The first example is done for you.

- value judgements by the reviewer, e.g.
  everything they do is just right
- use of specialist vocabulary
- vocabulary of description
- orientation (factual details of when, who, what, where)
- present tense to comment on the quality of a product
- proper nouns (names of people, places, titles).

Activity 4

Now write your own review of a performance, which you have seen live or on video, that you like or dislike. Try to include as many features of a review text as you can.

Knowledge about language Speech punctuation

Speech marks are used to mark the actual words someone speaks (direct speech). They are also used to quote someone's written words, including the titles of songs. Look at the extract below, which describes a conversation about Edinburgh's Hogmanay celebrations. Write out three sentences of direct speech that reflect the original conversation. An example is done for you.

I asked Iain if he was worried that Edinburgh's Hogmanay fireworks would be cancelled this year. He said he didn't think so, but if they were, he would enjoy the street party anyway. I asked him what his plans were and he said he had tickets for the concerts in the Gardens.

- 'Are you worried that Edinburgh's Hogmanay fireworks will be cancelled this year?' I asked Iain.

6 Carrying out research

You are learning:
• to consider different viewpoints on a topic.

Television is one of the most popular and influential forms of communication. Debates still rage among parents, social commentators and the media about the pros and cons of TV's influence on children.

Activity 1

Read the article below and write a paragraph to summarise the author's viewpoint in your own words.

How TV is (quite literally) killing us

by Dr Aric Sigman, *Daily Mail* 1 October 2005

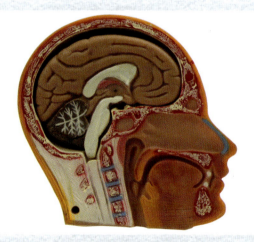

What, I wondered, would Baird make of TV now? What would he think of Jerry Springer's jeering mob? What would he make of television becoming more popular than shopping or going to the pub, church or library combined?

Or that more people would vote in a TV contest (*Pop Idol*) than for the Prime Minister and his entire party at the last election?

More pertinently, would he ever believe that his remarkable invention would come to represent one of the greatest dangers to the health of Britain and its social well-being at the dawn of the 21st century?

I've spent months poring over articles in journals ranging from *The Lancet* and *New England Journal of Medicine* to *Nature* and the *Journal of Neuroscience*.

The picture I formed was profoundly disturbing and amounts to what I believe to be the greatest health scandal of our time. I learned that viewing even moderate amounts of television:

• may damage brain cell development and function
• is the only adult pastime from the ages of 20 to 60 positively linked to developing Alzheimer's disease
• is a direct cause of obesity – a bigger factor even than eating junk food or taking too little exercise

Explanation

ADHD attention deficit hyperactivity disorder

- significantly increases the risk of Type 2 diabetes
- may biologically trigger premature puberty
- leads to a significantly elevated risk of sleep problems in adulthood, causing hormone changes which in turn increase body-fat production and appetite, damages the immune system and may lead to a greater vulnerability to cancer
- is a major independent cause of clinical depression (of which Britain has the highest rate in Europe).

These are not wild suppositions: they are based on hard, clinical evidence that has lain buried in academic journals.

For example, scientists at the University of Washington studied 2,500 children and found a strong link between early television exposure and attention problems by age seven which was 'consistent with a diagnosis of **ADHD**'.

For every hour of television a child watches a day, they noted a nine per cent increase in attentional damage.

Equally shocking was the report in the medical journal *Pediatrics*, which studied the metabolic rates of 31 children while undertaking a variety of activities and found that when they watched TV, the children burned the equivalent of 211 calories fewer per day than if they did absolutely nothing.

In Bhutan – the last country on earth to introduce TV – I was appalled to discover that since the arrival of 46 cable channels, the country was experiencing its first serious crime wave. Greed, avarice and selfishness had replaced traditional values of peace and respect.

Bhutanese academics had conducted a study which showed how television was to blame for increasing crime, corruption and dramatically changing attitudes to relationships.

They were particularly appalled to discover that more than a third of parents now preferred to watch television than talk to their own children.

Consider the facts. By the age of 75, most of us will have spent more than twelve-and-a-half years of 24-hour days watching television. It has become the industrialised world's main activity,

taking up more of our time than any other single activity except work and sleep.

Children now spend more time watching a television screen than they spend in school. At this very moment, the average six-year-old will have already watched television for nearly one full year of their lives.

When other screen-based viewing, such as computer games, is included, the figure is far higher. Children aged 11 to 15 now spend 53 hours a week watching TV and computers – an increase of 40 per cent in a decade.

The health implications for our children are particularly worrying with the finding that television viewing among children under three seems to damage their future learning abilities – permanently.

'the average six-year-old will have already watched television for nearly one full year'

The statistics bear this out. Children who have televisions in their bedrooms at ages eight and nine score worst in school achievement tests. And a 26-year study, tracking children from birth, has just concluded 'television viewing in childhood and adolescence is associated with poor educational achievement by 26 years of age'.

Significant long-term damage occurs even at so-called 'modest levels' of viewing – between one and two hours a day.

Confronted with such evidence, I would argue that reducing our screen time must now be a health priority.

Ultimately, people will have to decide for themselves how much and what type of television they and their children watch – but they must now be made aware that there is a dark side to John Logie Baird's 'seeing by wireless' machine.

Activity 2

1   How does the writer suggest that his point of view has been scientifically proven to be correct – and that we should believe and agree with him? Use evidence from the text to support your answer.

2   **a**   There are several points in the article about the negative effects of television. Does the writer mention any of its possible positive effects?

    b   Why do you think this is?

Activity 3

1   **a**   What do you think are the advantages of children watching television? Make a list of up to ten points, then choose your best three. An example has been done for you.

> • Children can learn information from factual programmes such as the news and documentaries.
>
> •

    b   Compare your best three advantages with a partner's. Discuss any similarities or differences.

2   In groups, devise and carry out a survey to assess:
   - the amount of TV watched by members of your class
   - the kinds of programmes they watch
   - their opinions on the points the article makes.

TV Questionnaire
1) How much TV do you watch on average per week?
   ☐ none   ☐ up to 5 hours
   ☐ up to 20 hours   ☐ over 20 hours

3   Record your research findings in an appropriate format such as a bar chart, pie chart or table. You will be using this information again in Section 7.

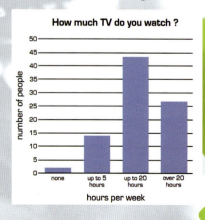

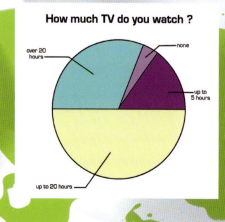

How much TV do you watch per week ?	Number of people
none	2
up to 5 hours	13
up to 20 hours	43
over 20 hours	27

Self-evaluation

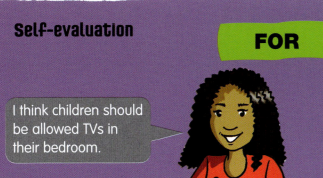

FOR

I think children should be allowed TVs in their bedroom.

AGAINST

I don't agree with children having TVs in their bedroom.

How confident are you about identifying arguments for and against? Make a copy of the table below and fill it in with two arguments for and two arguments against children having TVs in their bedroom. Try to fill in the table within 5 minutes, then identify your confidence level with your choices of argument by using the green, amber and red traffic lights next to your table.

not confident

quite confident

very confident

Points for TVs in children's bedrooms	Points against TVs in children's bedrooms

Knowledge about language Apostrophes for possession

Apostrophes are used to show that something belongs to or is connected with someone. The apostrophe should be positioned after the noun that defines that person, for example:

Andrew's pencil case.

The paragraph below is a student's description of her family's television-watching habits. Identify any errors in the use of apostrophes and write out the correct version.

Our familys television habits are quite varied. My sisters obsession is the soaps and because of this she probably watches about 9 hours of those per week, before you even start counting other programmes! My little brothers TV watching is much less. He is only 6 and my father limits his TV time. My parents watching habits are more difficult to comment on. My mother has the TV on in the kitchen a lot but isn't really watching it! My dads main love is his computer, but he watches about an hour of TV a night which is usually the news.

7 Presenting a balanced analysis

You are learning:
- to present a balanced analysis of an event or issue.

Some of us have strong points of view for or against a particular argument. However, there are many times in life when we need to make a compromise with people who have different views from our own.

Activity 1

Look back at the article on pages 24–25 and the feedback you gathered from members of your class in Activity 3 on page 26. Complete a table like the one below, listing as many relevant points as possible to summarise both sides of the argument.

For children watching TV	Against children watching TV

Activity 2

What compromises could you suggest to these parents which both of them might agree with? Write down three suggestions.

Activity 3

Read this letter from a concerned mother.

Dear Agony Aunt,

My husband was brought up in a family where they watched no TV. Our child is now 3 years old and has not had TV, which my husband and I agreed was the best way. However, I think this means I am having to care and play with him during all his waking hours and I'm exhausted without the break that many of my friends get when their child watches children's TV for an hour. I also wonder about the impact of this when he is older and at school. Can you give me your opinion about what I should do?

A concerned mother

Write three paragraphs of advice for the concerned mother, giving her a balanced outline of the issues and a viewpoint that would offer some compromise. You could use the following structure:

Paragraph 1: the negative side of children watching television.
Paragraph 2: the positive side of children watching television.
Paragraph 3: your suggestions for a compromise.

Knowledge about language Paragraphs

A paragraph is a group of sentences about one main idea. For example, a report about school ICT facilities might be made up of the five paragraphs listed opposite.

Write three paragraphs about your television-watching habits. Then give each paragraph a title that summarises the main idea it contains.

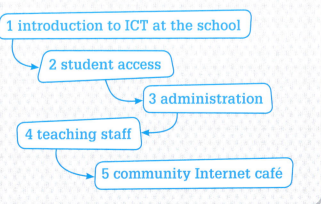

1 introduction to ICT at the school

2 student access

3 administration

4 teaching staff

5 community Internet café

Writing Activity
Functional writing

TV review

A newspaper is giving readers the opportunity to write a review of a programme or type of programme. This is the notice that appears in the paper.

> ## What do you watch? Soap operas? Football? Reality shows? Makeover programmes?
>
> We want readers' reviews of programmes explaining what they think is good about them and what they think the programme makers could do better.

Your task

Write a review of a television programme you have seen recently – or choose one to watch for this task.

Consider the programme's strengths and weaknesses. Is it trying to persuade you about something, tell a story or explore an issue? How well does it do it?

Structure your review around these strengths and weaknesses. Your introductory paragraph should give a brief explanation of what the programme is about. Then the following paragraphs should be based on a detailed analysis of particular strengths and weaknesses.

In your conclusion, explain whether you consider the strengths outweigh the weaknesses or the weaknesses outweigh the strengths. Give reasons for your views.

Look again at the key features of a review text on page 23 to help you.

You will be assessed on:
- your ability to give evaluative comments, supported by evidence on the programme you have chosen
- your organisation of your material in a way that is effective for your readers
- your sentence structure, paragraphing and spelling.

2 Short stories

Experiences and outcomes

In this unit you will:

Reading
- explore the ideas, viewpoints and themes in a variety of short stories
- read, explore and comment on a range of short story openings, conflicts, climaxes and endings
- comment on a writer's language choice and craft
- explore languages of Scotland.

Writing
- develop your writing skills by effectively selecting and structuring your ideas
- explore effective short story structures and use them to plan your own stories
- use a range of techniques and devices to develop your writing.

Talking and Listening
- discuss a range of texts
- discuss your own ideas for writing stories.

Words and sentences
- check verb tenses for accuracy
- use prepositions correctly
- learn when to start a new paragraph
- learn how to avoid overuse of pronouns.

By the end of this unit you will:

- analyse the text of an entire short story written in Scots (Reading Activity: Close reading)
- write your own short story (Writing Activity: Imaginative Writing).

1 Structure

Every story is different but almost all stories have one thing in common: they usually follow a similar structure, which helps to engage the reader and hold their attention.

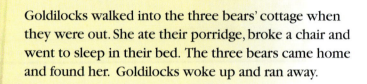

Activity 1

1 Read the story opposite. Did you enjoy it? Write one or two sentences giving reasons for your answer.

2 This version of 'Goldilocks' gives only the basic details. It has been reduced to four sentences, each of which covers one of the key elements of story structure:

> Goldilocks walked into the three bears' cottage when they were out. She ate their porridge, broke a chair and went to sleep in their bed. The three bears came home and found her. Goldilocks woke up and ran away.

Story structure elements	Description	Example from 'Goldilocks'
Set-up	The situation at the start of the story is established.	Sentence 1
Conflict	There is a problem.	Sentence 2
Climax	The problem reaches its worst point.	Sentence 3
Resolution	The problem is sorted out – sometimes happily.	Sentence 4

3 Think of a story you know well. It could be a favourite book or a folk tale, like 'Goldilocks'. Write the complete story in just four sentences. Label each sentence as either *set-up, conflict, climax* or *resolution*.

Activity 2

1 Read this *very* short story.

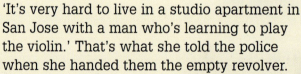

The Scarlatti Tilt

'It's very hard to live in a studio apartment in San Jose with a man who's learning to play the violin.' That's what she told the police when she handed them the empty revolver.

2 **a** Write a brief summary, explaining what happened.

b We are told some of the events in the story **directly**. Others are **implied**. In your summary, underline the **implied** events.

3 **a** Label the following in your story summary: set-up, conflict, climax and resolution.

b How could you add more detail to the story? Add your ideas around your four labels.

4 Write the opening paragraph of your new, detailed version of the story.

Activity 3

1 Look at these key events from a selection of stories.

Sees a knife on the floor

A woman is lost on the hills

A shot is fired

Hears footsteps

The police make an arrest

A girl is lying in bed

There's a fight

A smiling stranger approaches

A man leaps out of the darkness

Old friends are reunited

It was all a misunderstanding

A man is breaking into a house

a Which are 'set-ups'?
b Which are 'conflicts'?
c Which are 'climaxes'?
d Which are 'resolutions'?

2 Choose one set-up, one conflict, etc., to form a complete story structure.

3 Add some detail to your story structure. What else can you tell the reader about:
- the characters
- the setting
- the situation they are in
- what happens to them?

4 Write your story in the style of 'The Scarlatti Tilt', squeezing all four stages into just two sentences. Aim to *imply* some of the events in the story, rather than tell the reader about them directly.

Knowledge about language: Tenses

It's very easy to start a story in the past tense and suddenly find that you are writing in the present tense. It's important that you do not drift from one tense to the other.

The sentences below mix their tenses. Copy and correct them twice:
- once so they are all in the past tense
- once so they are all in the present tense.

1 She ran as fast as she could but they are still following her.
2 He was a man who believes everything he is told.
3 He sleeps all day and, at night, he worked a twelve-hour shift at the factory.
4 He reached the top of the ladder and, struggling to get his breath, finds he has an excellent view of the street below.

2 Openings

You are learning:
- to identify some of the different ways in which writers begin short stories.

Writers want to capture the reader's attention with the opening of their short story, but there are many ways of doing this. Sometimes writers use their opening to describe the scene, or to introduce characters or to intrigue the reader; and some writers jump straight in with the conflict to grab our attention.

Activity 1

1 Read this story opening. Then answer questions 2–4.

Death and the Boy
retold by Anthony Horowitz

West Africa was gripped by the unrelenting hand of famine. Its arid breath whispered over the land, blighting the crops and blistering the livestock. Its shadow fell across the villages, stretching even further in the remorseless sunlight. The water holes shrivelled and dried up. The mud hardened then cracked. Wherever the people went, black flies followed, sucking the last drops of moisture from the corners of their eyes and mouths.

2 How does this opening make you feel? Which words has the writer chosen to achieve this effect?

3 Which do you think is the most effective descriptive word in this opening? Why?

4 Look at these four words taken from the opening sentences:
   a What is the writer comparing the famine to?
   b What effect does this create?

gripped
hand
breath
shadow

Activity 2

1 Read this story opening. Then answer questions 2 and 3.

2 Do you think this is a good way to start the story?
   Write two or three sentences explaining your answer.

3 What things does this opening make you want to find out more about?

At the Edge of the Country
Alexander McCall Smith

'Little things,' once he said to his son. 'Little things change your life. Something that somebody just happens to say to you. Everything can be different after that.'
    Fraser had left Scotland in 1946, as a young man of eighteen.

Activity 3

1   Read this story opening. Then answer questions 2–5.

2   Do you think this is a good way to start the story? Write two or three sentences giving reasons for your answer.

3   What do we learn about the narrator of this story?

4   Describe the relationship between the narrator and her mother.

5   How does Janet Paisley try to make this seem like someone is speaking?

Killer Mum

Janet Paisley

See ma Mum. She's a killer. Gaun doon the toon tae git new docs. Middle ae wintur. Whit's she weerin? A woolly hat. I kid you not. Knittit gloves and a woolly hat. An hus the cheek tae walk aside me doon the street. Come oan. Mean tae say. Wid your Mum dae that?

Activity 4

1   Identify the techniques each of the writers in Activities 1–3 has used to grab the reader's attention. Use a table like the one below to record your answers.

Technique	Anthony Horowitz (page 34)	Alexander McCall Smith (page 34)	Janet Paisley (page 35)
The writer has described the scene.			
The writer has introduced characters.			
The writer has intrigued the reader.			
The writer has gone straight to the conflict.			
The writer has used dialogue.			

Hint: Some of the openings use more than one of these techniques.

2   Which one of the openings is most successful in making you want to read the rest of the story? Write two or three sentences explaining your answer.

3   Look back to the story you planned in Activity 3 on page 33. Write the opening few sentences using at least one of the above techniques.

Self-evaluation

Use this table to assess how effectively your story opening is written.

Beginner	Competent	Expert
I have used at least one of the techniques	I have used more than one of the techniques	I have used at least two techniques
I have used details to achieve the effect I want to have on the reader	I have chosen lots of detail to achieve the effect I want to have on the reader	I chose these, and every detail in my writing, to suit the effect I wanted to have on the reader

3 Characters

You are learning:
- to create effective characters for a story.

Stories need really interesting characters. There are many ways that writers can create a good character for a story. They might:
- create a character who is humorous
- create a character similar to the people who might read the story
- create a character the reader admires or finds interesting
- create a character the reader cares about
- create a character with some interesting flaws or problems that the reader wants to learn more about.

Activity 1

1 Think about the ways that the writer creates characters as you read extracts A–D below and on page 37.

A

from Hurricane Jack

Neil Munro

I very often hear my friend the Captain speak of Hurricane Jack in terms of admiration and devotion, which would suggest that Jack is a sort of demigod. The Captain always refers to Hurricane Jack as the most experienced seaman of modern times, as the most fearless soul that ever wore oilskins, the handsomest man in Britain, so free with his money that he would fling it at the birds, so generally accomplished that it would be a treat to be left a month on a desert island alone with him.

B

from Silver Linings

Joan Lingard

Every cloud is supposed to have one, or so I learned at my granny's knee. Isn't that where you are supposed to learn such things? My granny is full of sayings, most of them rubbish according to my mother, who has her own sayings. Like most mothers. My granny isn't one of those grandmothers who sits and knits in the chimney corner, shrouded in shawls, if such grannies exist at all. She tints her hair auburn and is employed as a manageress in the local supermarket. It's not all that 'super' I must add, as it's only got two aisles, one up and one down, but still a job's a job these days. And money doesn't grow …

Money's a problem in our family and my granny helps us keep afloat with 'care' parcels. She dumps them down on the kitchen table muttering about the improvidence of my parents and the wasted education of my mother who had all the chances in life that she didn't have herself.

C

from Mary Moon and the Stars

Janice Galloway

Mary Moon was as thin as a string, white-yellow hair hanging down her back in rats' tails. She had specs with elasticated legs and her socks sometimes didn't match. Her skin was see-through and she smelled like a cat's cushion. She sat next to George Dickie who kept nipping folk. There were always marks on her arms. My mother said she was a Poor Soul and told me to ask her round for her tea but I didn't. I suppose I was scared of the rings under her eyes, her fingernails always needing cut. I told myself she wouldn't come anyway and just didn't bother.

D

from A Time to Dance

Bernard MacLaverty

Nelson, with a patch over one eye, stood looking idly into Mothercare's window. The sun was bright behind him and made a mirror out of the glass. He looked at his patch with distaste and felt it with his finger. The elastoplast was rough and dry and he disliked the feel of it. Bracing himself for the pain, he ripped it off and let a yell out of him. A woman looked down at him curiously to see why he had made the noise but by that time he had the patch in his pocket. He knew without looking that some of his eyebrow would be on it.

2 **a** Do you find these characters interesting? Why?
   b Which of the techniques listed on page 36 have the authors used to create these characters? Are any techniques used in these texts not included in the list on page 36? Copy and complete the table below.

Story	Techniques used
Hurricane Jack	
Silver Linings	
Mary Moon and the Stars	
A Time to Dance	

3 Which of these characters are you most interested in? Write two or three sentences explaining your answer.

Knowledge about language Prepositions

He climbed <u>over</u> the wall, <u>under</u> the hedge, and ran <u>towards</u> the house <u>before</u> coming to a sudden halt.

The underlined words are prepositions. They come before a noun phrase and give information about time, place and direction.

1 Sort the prepositions in the bank into three categories: time, place and direction.

2 Choose prepositions from that bank that could be used to complete these sentences:
   a He fell _____ his bed and went to sleep.
   b You shouldn't eat a big meal _____ swimming.
   c He hid the key _____ the doormat.

Preposition bank

off	into	over
under	above	around
in	before	after
while	during	near

4 Point of view

You are learning:
- how writers use the first person narrative voice to create a character.

A story can be told from many points of view. When the story is being told to us by one of the characters actually in the story it is called **first person narrative**. The advantage of telling a story using first person narrative is that the narrator can directly tell us his or her feelings and opinions. Many stories are written in third person narrative. This is when the narrator is someone telling the story from outside. With third person narrative we can be told the feelings and thoughts of many characters.

Activity 1

1   Read the extract below and answer the questions that follow.

from She

Rosa Guy

'Just where do you think you're going?' she said.

'To the bathroom,' I said.

'No you're not,' she said. 'Not before you wash up these dishes.'

'This is a matter of urgent necessity,' I said. I hated that even going to my bedroom had to be questioned.

'Don't want to hear,' she said. 'I'm sick and tired of emergency, emergency, every night after dinner. Get to that sink.'

'I'll wash the dishes,' Linda said. She got up and started to clear off the table. I slipped out of the kitchen. The angry voice followed me down the hall:

'Linda, don't keep letting your sister get away with everything.'

'I don't mind, really, Dorine,' Linda said.

'That girl's just too damn lazy …' I shut the bathroom door to muffle the sounds of her grievances against me. She didn't like me. She never had. And I didn't care. Stepmothers …!

2   **a**   How does the narrator feel about her stepmother?

    b   How do we know? Think about what the narrator has chosen to tell us about her stepmother, and the way she describes her own feelings.

Activity 2

1 Read the extract opposite and answer the questions that follow.

The narrator is a school girl who has been asked by her attractive house captain if she will run in the school games.

2 How does the narrator feel when she is asked to take part? How do you know this?

3 Explain how she tries to control her emotions.

4 Why do you think she accepts?

from The Cure
Liz Lochhead

He goes: Aha the very one I've been looking for.

I'm like, who me? Feeling this big beamer of a riddy creep up to my face. Trying to do a mind over matter over blushing.

He goes: Gemma, the very girl. Listen, Gems, your gonny run in the Intermediate Inter-house Mixed Relay, right?

I'm like that.

…

Nuh. No way Ho-zay. I'm no daen it. That's what I should of says. All I get out, but, is: I canny … *please* don't … don't ask me.

He got round us. Dead easy. Would not take no for an answer. Pardon. I didn't catch that. You see I need you, Gemma, simple as that. You're running.

Activity 3

You are going to invent a character to be used in a short story. Use this flowchart to develop your character and help to establish them in your mind. You could use bullet points or a mind-map at this stage of planning.

1 What is your character's name and age?

2 Write down a few basic details of your character's situation.

3 What does your character look like? What is he or she wearing?

4 What kind of personality does your character have? Think about what would make him or her unique and interesting.

Activity 4

1 Write a short extract similar to the ones on pages 36–37. Use your notes from Activity 3 to help you write about your character in proper sentences. Don't worry about developing a story situation at this stage. The aim is to present an interesting character. You can write your extract in the first or third person narrative voice.

2 Let someone else read your extract. Ask them to give you feedback on:
   ● what they found effective about your description
   ● what they found interesting about your character.

5 Conflict and climax

You are learning:
- how writers develop their stories.

One of the reasons we have always told stories is that we love to hear about problems – preferably other people's problems! – and how they are resolved. An effective story needs some kind of conflict or problem to trigger the narrative – to get the story started – and fire the reader's interest.

The word **conflict** is often used to describe some kind of physical confrontation. In stories, however, it does not need to mean this. Some examples of conflicts in stories are:
- the relationship between characters
- a problem that a character has to overcome or try to resolve
- an internal conflict where a character struggles with their own conscience
- a conflict of ideas.

As the conflict grows to its **climax**, or most dramatic part, so does the reader's interest.

Activity 1

1 Read extracts A–C. They are taken from the early part of short stories in which the writer triggers the narrative with conflict.

In Ralph Prince's story 'Sharlo's Strange Bargain', Sharlo meets a stranger.

A

Sharlo asked him who he was, and the man said that everybody knew him. Sharlo then looked at him closely to see if he really knew him. The man seemed neither young nor old, but ageless. His skin was red and looked like the skin of a boiled lobster. His hair was white and flowing. His eyes were red, and they glowed as if fires burned within them. 'Never seen you before,' said Sharlo, after looking at him searchingly and long.

'You will soon remember who I am,' declared the man, 'and you will get to know me more, Sharlo.'

'How you know me name?' asked Sharlo, in surprise.

B

In Brian McCabe's story 'Kreativ Riting', the teacher Mr Pitcairn (PK) is trying to get his class to settle and do some writing. They don't really seem able or willing to start.

'Try and use a bit of imagination!' PK says. Then he stops at my desk and looks at me and says, 'If you've got one, I mean. You have got an imagination, Joe, haven't you?'

This is him slaggin' me, ken?

So I says, 'Naw, sir, but I've got a video.'

That got a laugh, ken?

So then PK says, 'The only trouble with you, Joe, is your head is choc-a-bloc with those videos and those video nasties. Those video nasties are worse than anything for your brain, Joe.'

Then Lenny Turnbull, who sits behind me and who is a poser, says: 'What brain? Joe's not got a brain in there, sir, just a bitty fresh air between his lugs!'

In Anne MacLeod's story 'Leaving Assynt', the reader is presented with the story of a troubled relationship.

C

It was breakfast, Sunday morning. Mary turned to Iain.

'You're off, then?' she asked.

He nodded.

'See you later.'

'No, I won't be here.'

'Suit yourself,' he said, slinging the rucksack over his shoulder. 'I'll be off the hill at five. I'll phone.'

'I won't be here,' she said again.

He shrugged. The front door banged.

Mary drained her coffee, and stood up slowly, carefully. Her back was sore, but she had a lot to do. She left the dishes lying on the breakfast bar, Iain's greasy plate, now empty of bacon and black pudding; her own more modest, sticky with marmalade. If he could ignore the dishes so could she.

2 a For each extract, write a sentence or two describing the problem or conflict the characters are facing. Is there just a single conflict in each story or can you see more than one possibility?

   b How do you think the conflict might develop in each of the extracts? Think of the kind of story or **genre** that the story is.

   c For each extract, predict the climax towards which the problem could build.

Explanation

genre a particular type or category of story. Some examples of genre are: science fiction; adventure; real-life fiction; fantasy; horror.

Activity 2

Read the following extract from the beginning of a story through to its climax. Think about how the conflict is developing as you read it.

Saskatchewan

by Lorn Macintyre

It's Games Day. The sun has risen over the bay and is coming through my cotton curtains, laying a golden quilt on my bed. I hear Father crossing the landing, then the rasp of his razor as he shaves, singing a Gaelic song. He is secretary of the Games and he knows that everything is ready on the field above the town. The marquees
5   that came on the cargo boat have been erected; the latrines dug. He rinses his razor under the tap and I hear the Old Spice I gave him for his Christmas being slapped on. Mother is up now, going down to the kitchen.

    I go to the corner of my bedroom and lift up the two swords. They have authentic looking hilts, but the blades are made of silver-painted wood. I cross them on the
10 carpet and lace up my pumps. Today I am dancing at the Games, and this year I hope to win the sword dance. I have been practising all winter, making the floor of my bedroom vibrate, with Mother claiming that the ceiling in the sitting-room will come down on top of her as she watches a soap on our temperamental set which sometimes has to be slapped to restore the signal. But Father came up to watch me dancing,
15 sitting on the bed as I danced by the window over my dud swords.

    'I'll be amazed if you don't win it this year, Marsali.'

    It's Games morning and I'm practising, landing on my toes as softly as possible to save them for the competition. Soon Mother will call up that breakfast is ready, but I will eat nothing more than a brown egg because I have seen competitors in previous
20 years throwing up behind the marquee.

I know where Father is. He is at the sitting-room window, watching for the dark blue bow of the steamer to slide up to the pier. It left one of the islands at dawn and is packed with spectators for the Games. Many of them are Father's customers in the bank, but that isn't why I hear the door closing as he goes down to the pier to wait by the gangway.

25 It's for the pleasure of hearing the Gaelic of another island spoken. I have put my swords away and can see the first of the spectators coming along the street from my high window. The men have raincoats folded over their shoulders and caps pushed to the backs of their heads as they look into the window of Black the ironmonger's. Their stout wives are at the other window where knitting needles are crossed in balls of wool.

30 The procession up to the field **musters** at the memorial clock and is led by the laird with a plaid over his shoulder and a long stick. The pipe band behind him is followed by the spectators, going up past the aromatic wild roses on the back brae. But I am already on the field, my number pinned to my frilled blouse. I have on my pumps and am practising in the subdued coolness of the tent, using my swords. Mothers are

35 fussing round other competitors, straightening the pleats of kilts and exhorting them to dance as well as they can.

A girl comes in. She is pretty, with a blue velvet bonnet angled on her blonde hair, and a plaid, held at her shoulder by a cairngorm brooch, trailing at her heels. She is carrying a holdall that says Canadian Pacific, and in her other hand she has two large swords.

40 'Hi,' she says to us all, and comes across to the corner of the tent where I am exercising to make my toes supple. 'I'm Jeannie Maclean.'

I go into my bag and check the programme. There is no such name down for the sword dance. She sees me looking at her quizzically and she says 'I'm a late entry. Mom posted the form a month ago but it never reached here. I went to see the secretary and

45 he says I can compete since I've come such a long way.'

'Where are you from?' I ask.

'Saskatchewan.'

Explanation

musters gathers

Immediately that name takes on a romantic resonance and I want her to say it again.

'It's in Canada,' she informs me, lacing up her pumps. 'We have wheat fields that
50 go on for miles.'

I am trying to imagine the ripe golden crop waving in the breeze when she adds
more information. 'Our people came from this island.'

'From here?' I say, surprised.

'U-huh. They were cleared last century and they found their way to Saskatchewan.
55 They did pretty well. We have four combine harvesters on our farm and my father has a
herd of Aberdeen Angus he shipped across.' It's not a boast but a factual statement.

'Are they real swords?' I enquire, reaching across to touch them.

'Claymores. My folks brought them across from this island. My grandfather said
we fought with them at Culloden.'
60 'If they came from here they must have spoken Gaelic,' I say.

'Sure, but we lost it when we intermarried. My great-grandmother was a squaw. I'd
love to learn Gaelic.' (She pronounces it Gale-ick.) 'Do you speak it?'

I nod, but I'm getting too involved in this conversation instead of preparing for the
competition. She, after all, is a rival, and as she lays the swords on the turf and begins
65 a practice dance, I see how good she is. She's dancing as she converses with me, her
shadow turning on the canvas wall of the tent. 'I've been doing this since I was three,
first with two wooden spoons on the floor of the kitchen. I need to win today. Mom's
outside.'

I don't want to stay in the tent to watch her practise because it's undermining my
70 confidence, so I go over the hill, past the latrines, already busy with early drinkers, to
a quiet hollow where I lay down my swords in the hum of insects and make my own
music with my mouth to dance to. But I feel there is something lacking. My feet are
heavy and I am aware of the clumsiness of my hands above my head. As I turn, my
foot touches a blade, and I stop, upset.
75 I hear Father's voice through the megaphone calling the competitors for the sword
dance. As I go back over the hill I feel he has betrayed me by letting the girl from
Saskatchewan – I am beginning to hate the name – enter for the competition when the
rule says entries in advance. The dancing judges from the mainland are sitting in the shade
of a lean-to beside the platform, with paper to mark the competitors on the card tables
80 above their knees. I sit on the hill to watch, but I am not impressed by the standard.

'Number 79, Jeannie Maclean.'

She comes up on to the platform with her swords under her arm and there is a
confab among the judges. Yes, she can use her own swords, as long as the steward lays
them down. He makes them into a cross for her on the boards. She puts her hands on
85 her hips and bows to the judges as the pipes tune up. I see from the first steps what
a beautiful dancer she is. I am watching her toes and they hardly seem to touch the
boards, springing in the air above the blades, now touching a diced stocking. The
people around me on the hillside are enthralled. To my left there is a woman also
wearing a Maclean kilt, with a cape. She is standing, holding up her thumbs to her
90 dancing daughter.

Jeannie Maclean is turning in the air, her kilt swirling. She is twenty seconds off the
trophy which is waiting on a table in the secretary's tent. Four nights ago I watched
father polishing it, and he told me: 'Your name will be on this, Marsali.'

Activity 3

1 Copy the table below and use it to show how this story develops.

Set-up	The situation at the start of the story is established.	
Conflict	There is a problem.	
Climax	The problem reaches its worst point.	

2 Describe the atmosphere in the set-up of the story. Which words and phrases help to create this?

3 How does the narrator feel about her chances in the competition? What has made her feel this way?

4 What details does the writer include to show that the day is important to more than just herself?

5 Marsali has mixed feelings about Jeannie Maclean when she meets her. There are certain things about Jeannie she likes and some she could dislike. Make a table like the one below highlighting these.

Reasons to like Jeannie	Things Marsali might dislike about her

6 How has the meeting between the two girls affected Marsali? Compare this with how she felt at the start of the story.

7 a Look at the words and phrases used to describe Jeannie's dancing. How do they create a sense of tension?
   b What other details add to the tension of this climax?
   c How does Marsali feel when Jeannie is dancing?

8 Is the confrontation over? What do you think still has to happen in the story?

6 Endings

You are learning:
- how to create an effective ending for a short story.

Endings are important. No matter how good the build-up is, a disappointing resolution may spoil the whole story for the reader. The ending is the last thing your reader will read, and the first thing they will remember about your story.

Activity 1

Writers can choose from a variety of different endings. Think of a story or film that uses one of these resolutions:

Activity 2

Look at extracts A and B, which are both story endings. What kind of resolution has each writer chosen to use? Remember: they may combine more than one kind of resolution.

- a twist – a surprise to make you think again about the rest of the story
- humour – like a joke, the end of the story has a punch line to make you laugh
- a moral – the story tries to teach us something about the characters and our own lives
- justice – the characters get what they deserve
- a different kind of ending
- a mystery or enigma – the ending of the story is never made entirely clear.

A

Saskatchewan

by Lorn Macintyre

Jeannie Maclean is performing her last movement when she comes down, heavily. I see the side of the pump touch the blade which slices through the leather. She is lying on the boards, holding her bleeding foot, and her mother is shouting behind me instead of going down to her injured daughter. 'You damn fool!'

Father calls for Dr MacDiarmid through the megaphone and he comes in his Bermuda shorts with his medical bag. Jeannie Maclean is helped off the platform and hops to the first-aid tent, her hand on the doctor's shoulder, to have her foot stitched.

It's my turn to dance and I turn to bow to the judges in the lean-to. How dearly now do I wish that the trophy for the sword dance was going across the ocean to Canada, to sit in a glass case in a prairie house where Gaelic was once spoken. But Jeannie Maclean is out of the competition. As my

toes touch the boards I am dancing to the refrain: Sas-katch-ew-an, Sas-katch-ew-an. I see Father crossing the field, his secretary's rosette on his lapel. He has come to watch me and he stands, smiling in encouragement. I know I have never danced better because this is a performance for him. Sas-katch-ew-an, Sas-katch-ew-an. I am reaching for the sky. Mother is on the hillside waving but she has never really been interested in Highland Dancing or Gaelic because she's from the mainland.

I can feel my toes so sure, as they come down between the blades. I turn to face my father, my knuckles on my hips. This is for you, Father, for all the patience and love, for the Gaelic words you give me. I turn to face the marquee. I can see a slumped shadow on the canvas, another shadow hanging over it, an arm raised. This is for you, Jeannie Maclean, with your wounded foot, your treacherous swords and your angry mom. I have nothing but pity and love, and as I bow to the judges and the applause rises I know that one day I will go to Saskatchewan.

The teacher Mr Pitcairn (PK) has had a difficult lesson trying to get his disruptive class to do some creative writing. The narrator, Joe, has decided to hand in his essay.

B

Kreativ Riting

by Brian McCabe

So here it is. This is my kreativ writing:

MY OWN SELF AS OTHERS SEE ME.

MY NAME IS JOE MURDOCH AND I AM SHEER MENTAL SO WATCH OUT. I HAVE GOT A GREEN MOHAWK. IT HAS GOT SCARLET SPIKES. ON MY FOREHEAD I HAVE GOT A SKULL AND CROSS-BONES. ON MY BLACK LEATHER JACKET I HAVE GOT 200 CHROME STUDS NOT COUNTING THE STUDS ON MY BELT AND MY DOG COLLAR. ON MY NECK I HAVE GOT A TATTOO IT SAYS CUT ALONG THE DOTTED LINE. ON MY BACK I HAVE GOT NO FUTURE. ON MY BOOTS I HAVE GOT NO HOPE. IN MY POCKET I HAVE GOT NO MONEY. MY MUM LOVES ME AND I LOVE HER BACK. MY DAD STOLE THE LEAD OFF THE DALKEITH EPISCOPALIAN CHURCH ROOF AND I GAVE HIM A HAND AND WE DIDN'T GET CAUGHT. I AM A WARRIOR AND I AM SHEER MENTAL SO WATCH OUT OK. THE END

And now I will take it out to PK and tell him I don't want to read it out to the class, and I don't want him to read it either. I will tell him that I want it to be *destroyed*. That should get a laugh, ken?

Activity 3

Write a description of the way that the writer has ended each of the stories in Activity 2. How do you think each writer wants the reader to feel at the end of their story? Use some evidence from the story in your answer.

Knowledge about language **Paragraphs**

There are four reasons for starting a new paragraph:
- a new scene or setting
- a new subject
- a new time
- a new speaker.

Copy the text below, putting it into paragraphs and labelling the reason for each new paragraph.

Danny sat at home, staring at his homework. English was not his favourite subject. 'I have no idea how to put paragraphs in this writing,' he said. He scratched his head and sighed. Meanwhile, his dad was downstairs, making a cup of tea. 'Danny!' his dad called up the stairs. 'I'm in my room,' Danny called back, 'trying to do my homework!'

Self-evaluation

You have been learning about a writer's decisions in structuring and writing short stories. Use this table to assess how well you are doing.

Beginner	Competent	Expert
I can comment on how a writer ends a story	I can comment in detail on the writer's decisions and their effect on the reader	I can analyse the writer's decisions and their contribution to the effect the writer intends to have on the reader

Reading Activity
Close reading

In the following story 'All That Glisters', by the Glaswegian writer Anne Donovan, a young girl has to deal with strong emotions. You will study how the story is skilfully written and structured.

Your task

Read the story, then answer the questions on page 53.

All That Glisters

Anne Donovan

Thon wee wifey brung them in, the wan that took us for two days when Mrs McDonald wis aff. She got us tae make Christmas cards wi coloured cardboard and felties, which is a bit much when we're in second year, but naebody wis gonnae say anything cos it's better than daein real work. Anyway

5   ah like daein things like that and it made a right neat wee card for ma daddy wi a Christmas tree and a robin and a bit a holly on it.

    That's lovely dear. What's your name?

    Clare.

    Would you like to use the glitter pens?

10   And she pulled oot the pack fae her bag.

  Ah'd never seen them afore. When ah wis in Primary Four the teacher gied us tubes of glitter but it was quite messy. Hauf the stuff ended up on the flair and it wis hard to make sure you got the glue in the right places. But these pens were different cos the glue wis mixed in with the glitter so

15   you could just draw with them. It was pure brilliant, so it wis. There wis four colours, rid, green, gold and silver, and it took a wee while tae get the hang of it. You had to be careful when you squeezed the tube so's you didnae get a blob appearin at wanst, but efter a few goes ah wis up and runnin.

  And when ah'd finished something amazing hud happened. Ah cannae

20   explain whit it wis but the glitter just brought everything tae life, gleamin and glisterin against the flat cardboard. It wis like the difference between a Christmas tree skinklin wi fairy lights an wan lying deid and daurk in a corner.

  Ma daddy wis dead chuffed. He pit the card on the bedside table and smiled.

25   *Fair brightens up this room hen.*

  It's good tae find sumpn that cheers him up even a wee bit because ma daddy's really sick. He's had a cough fur as long as ah can remember, and he husny worked for years, but these past three months he cannae even get oot his bed. Ah hear him coughing in the night sometimes and

30   it's different fae the way he used to cough, comes far deeper inside him somehow, seems tae rack his hale body fae inside oot. When ah come in

fae school ah go and sit wi him and tell him about whit's happened that day, but hauf the time he looks away fae me and stares at a patch on the downie cover where there's a coffee stain that ma ma cannae wash oot. He used tae work
35 stripping oot buildings and he wis breathing in stoor aw day, sometimes it wis that bad he'd come hame wi his hair and his claes clairtit wi it. He used tae kid on he wis a ghost and walk in the hoose wi his airms stretched out afore him an ah'd rin and hide unner the stair, watching him walk by wi the faint powdery whiteness floatin roon his head.

40   He never knew there wis asbestos in the dust, never knew a thing about it then, nane of them did. Noo he's an expert on it, read up aw these books tae try and unnerstaun it fur the compensation case. Before he got really sick he used tae talk aboot it sometimes.

    You see, hen, the word asbestos comes fae a Greek word that means
45 *indestructible. That's how they use it fur fireproofin – the fire cannae destroy it.*

    You mean that if you wore an asbestos suit you could walk through fire and it widnae hurt you?

    Aye in the aulden days they used tae bury the royals in it. They cried it the funeral dress of kings.

* * *

50   The next day the wee wumman let me use the pens again. Sometimes when you think something's brilliant it disnae last, you get fed up wi it dead quick and don't know why you wanted it in the first place. But the pens werenae like that, it wis even better than the first time cos ah knew whit to dae with them. Yesterday ah'd put the glitter on quite thick in a solid block a colour, but today
55 ah found a different way a daein it almost by accident. Ah'd drawn a leaf shape and coloured it green but a bit squirted out intae a big blob, so ah blotted it and when ah took the paper away the shape that wis left wis nicer than the wan ah'd made deliberately. The outline wis blurred and the glitter wis finer and lighter, the colour of the card showing through so it looked as if sumbudy'd
60 sprinkled it, steady ladelin it on; looked cracking. The teacher thought so too.

    It's lovely, Clare. It's more … subtle.

Subtle, ah liked that word.

    Ah tellt ma daddy about it that night efter school, sittin on the chair beside his bed. He seemed a bit better than usual, mair alert, listenin tae whit ah hud tae
65 say, but his skin wis a terrible colour and his cheeks were hollow.

    Whit did she mean, subtle, hen? How wis it subtle?

    Ah tried tae think of the words tae explain it, but ah couldnae. Ah looked at ma fingers which were covered in glitter glue and then at ma daddy's haun lyin on the bedcover, bones stickin out and veins showin through. Ah took his haun
70 in mines and turnt it roon so his palm faced upwards.

    Look, daddy.

    Ah showed him the middle finger of ma right haun, which was thick wi solid gold, then pressed doon on his palm. The imprint of ma finger left sparkly wee trails a light.
75   He smiled a wavery wee smile.

Aye, hen, subtle.

That night ah lay awake fur a while imagining aw the things ah could dae wi the glitter pens. Ah really wanted tae make sumpn for ma daddy's Christmas wi them. The tips of ma fingers were still covered in glitter, and they sparkled in
80 the daurk. Ah pressed ma fingers aw over the bedclothes so they gleamed in the light fae the streetlamp outside, then ah fell intae a deep glistery sleep.

***

£3.49 for a pack of four. An ah hud wan ninety-three in ma purse.

Ah lifted the pack and went tae the check-oot.

Much are they?

85 *Three forty-nine.*

Aye, but much are they each?

The wummin at the till hud dyed jet-black hair and nae eyebrows.

We don't sell them individually.

She spat oot the word *individually* as if it wis sumpn disgusting.

90 *Aye but you'll get mair fur them. Look, you can have wan ninety-three for two.*

Ah've already tellt you that we don't sell them individually, ah cannae split the pack.

Ah could see there wis nae point in arguin wi her so ah turnt roon and walked towards the shelf tae pit them back. If Donna'd been wi me, she'd
95 have just knocked them. She's aye taking sweeties an rubbers an wee things like that. She's that casual about it, she can just walk past a shelf and wheech sumpn intae her pocket afore anyone notices, never gets caught. And she's that innocent-lookin, wi her blonde frizzy curls an her neat school uniform naebody wid guess tae look at her she wis a tea-leaf.

100 She's aye on tae me tae dae it, but ah cannae. A suppose it's cos of ma ma and da, they're dead agin thieving. Donna widnae rob hooses or steal sumpn oot yer purse but she disnae think stealin oot a shop is stealin. A lot of folk think like that. Donna's big brother Jimmy tried tae explain tae me that it wis ok tae steal ooty shops cos they made such big profits that they werenae really stealing
105 affy us (the working classes he cries us though he husny worked a day in his life) and they're aw insured anyway so it disnae matter. Even though ah can see the sense in whit Jimmy's sayin, well, ma daddy says stealin is stealin, and ah cannae go against his word.

In the end ah sellt ma dinner ticket tae big Maggie Hughes and all week
110 ah wis starving for ah only hud an apple or a biscuit ma ma gied me fur a playpiece. But on Friday it was worth it when ah went doon the shops at lunchtime tae buy the pens. It was a different wumman that served me and she smiled as she pit them in a wee plastic poke.

Are you gonnae make Christmas decorations, hen?

115 *Ah'm no sure.*

Ah got some fur ma wee boy an he loved them.

Aye, they're dead good. Thanks.

***

Ah couldny wait tae show them off tae ma da, but as soon as ah opened the door of the hoose ah knew there wis sumpn wrang. It wis that quiet, nae telly, nae
120 radio on in the kitchen. Ma mammy wis sittin on the settee in the livin room.

Her face wis white and there were big black lines under her eyes.

Mammy, whit's . . .

C'mere, hen, sit doon beside me.

She held her weddin ring between the thumb and first finger of her right
125 haun, twistin it roon as she spoke and ah saw how loose it wis on her finger. No
long ago it wis that tight she couldnae get it aff.

Clare, yer daddy had a bad turn jist this afternoon and we had tae go tae the
hospital wi him. Ah'm awful sorry, hen, ah don't know how tae tell you, but your
daddy's died.

130 Ah knew it wis comin, ah think ah'd known since ah walked intae the hoose,
but when she said the words the coldness shot though me till ah felt ma bones
shiverin and ah heard a voice, far away in anither room, shoutin but the shouts
were muffled as if in a fog, and the voice wis shoutin *naw, naw, naw!*

And ah knew it wis ma voice.

135 We sat there, ma mammy and me, her airms roond me, till ah felt the warmth
of her body gradually dissolve the ice of mine. Then she spoke, quiet and soft.

Now, hen, you know that this is fur the best, no fur us but fur yer daddy.

Blue veins criss-crossed the back of her haun. Why were veins blue when
blood wis red?

140 *You know your daddy'd no been well fur a long time. He wis in a lot of pain,*
and he wisnae gonnae get better. At least this way he didnae suffer as much.
He's at peace noo.

We sat for a long time, no speakin, just haudin hauns.

***

The funeral wis on the Wednesday and the days in between were a blur of folk
145 comin an goin, of makin sandwiches and drinking mugs of stewed tea, saying
rosaries and pourin out glasses of whisky for men in overcoats. His body came
hame tae the hoose and wis pit in the bedroom. Ma mammy slept in the bed
settee in the livin room wi ma Auntie Pauline.

Are you sure that you want tae see him?

150 Ah wis sure. Ah couldnae bear the fact we'd never said goodbye and kept
goin ower and ower in ma mind whit ah'd have said tae him if ah'd known he
wis gonnae die so soon. Ah wis feart as well, right enough. Ah'd never seen a
dead body afore, and ah didnae know whit tae expect, but he looked as if he wis
asleep, better in fact than he looked when he wis alive, his face had mair colour,
155 wis less yella lookin and lined. Ah sat wi him for a while in the room, no saying
anything, no even thinking really, just sittin. Ah felt that his goin wis incomplete
and ah wanted tae dae sumpn fur him, but that's daft, whit can ye dae when
sumbdy's deid? Ah wondered if ah should ask ma mammy but she was that
withdrawn intae herself, so busy wi the arrangements that ah didnae like tae.
160 She still smiled at me but it was a watery far away smile and when she kissed
me goodnight ah felt she wis haudin me away fae her.

On the Wednesday mornin ah got up early, got dressed and went through tae
the kitchen. Ma Auntie Pauline wis sittin at the table havin a cuppa tea and a
fag. When she looked up her face froze over.

165 *Whit the hell dae you think you're daein? Go and get changed this minute.*
But these are ma best claes.
You cannae wear red tae a funeral. You have to show respect for the deid.
But these were ma daddy's favourites. He said ah looked brilliant in this.
Ah mind his face when ah came intae the room a couple of month ago, after
170 ma mammy'd bought me this outfit fur ma birthday; a red skirt and a zip-up
jacket wi red tights tae match.
You're a sight for sore eyes, hen.
That sounds horrible, daddy.
He smiled at me.
175 *It disnae mean that, hen. It means you look that nice you would make sore*
eyes feel better. Gie's a twirl, princess.
An ah birled roon on wan leg, laughin.

***

Thae claes are no suitable for a funeral.
Ah'm gonnae ask ma mammy.
180 Ah turned to go oot the room.
Don't you dare disturb your mother on a day like this tae ask her aboot claes.
Have you no sense? Clare, you're no a baby, it's time you grew up and showed
some consideration for other folk. Get back in that room and put on your school
skirt and sweatshirt and your navy-blue coat. And ah don't want to hear
185 *another word about this.*
In the bedroom ah threw masel intae a corner and howled ma heid aff. The
tears kept comin and comin till ah felt ah wis squeezed dry and wid never be
able tae shed anither tear. Ah took aff the red claes and changed intae ma grey
school skirt and sweatshirt and pit ma navy-blue coat ower it. Ah looked at
190 masel in the full-length mirror in the middle of the wardrobe and saw this dull
drab figure, skin aw peely-wally. Ma daddy wid have hated to see me like this
but ah didnae dare go against ma auntie's word.
The only bit of me that had any life aboot it wis ma eyes fur the tears had
washed them clean and clear. A sunbeam came through the windae and ah
195 watched the dustspecks dancing in its light. There was a hair on the collar of ma
coat and it lit up intae a rainbow of colours. As ah picked it up and held it in ma
fingers, an idea came to me. Ah went tae ma schoolbag which had been left lyin
in the corner of the room since Friday, took oot ma glitter pens and unwrapped
them. Ah took the gold wan, squeezin the glitter on ma fingers then rubbin it
200 intae ma hair, then added silver and red and green. The strands of hair stood
oot roon ma heid like a halo, glisterin and dancin in the light. Ah covered the
dull cloth so it was bleezin wi light, patterns scattered across it, even pit some
on ma tights and ma shoes. Then ah pressed ma glittery fingers on ma face,
feelin ma cheekbones and eyebrows and the soft flesh of ma mouth and the
205 delicate skin of ma eyelids. And ah felt sad for a moment as ah thought of the
deid flesh of ma daddy, lyin alone in the cold church. Then ah stood and looked
in the mirror at the glowin figure afore me and ah smiled.
Subtle, daddy?
Aye, hen, subtle.

1 Read from the beginning of the story to the line of dialogue 'Fair brightens up this room hen' (lines 1–25). How would you describe the mood at this part of the story? Which ideas, words and phrases create this mood?

2 Look at the description of Clare's father in lines 26–49. How does this change the mood of the story? Explain your answer using evidence from the text.

3 How does the writer show a close relationship between Clare and her father? In your answer you should comment on:
   ● the things that they do
   ● what they say to each other
   ● how they speak to each other.

4 In lines 82–117, what problem does Clare face? How does she overcome this?

5 Look at the paragraph below from the story. How does the atmosphere in the story change at this point?

> Ah couldny wait tae show them off tae ma da, but as soon as ah opened the door of the hoose ah knew there wis sumpn wrang. It wis that quiet, nae telly, nae radio on in the kitchen. Ma mammy wis sittin on the settee in the livin room. Her face wis white and there were big black lines under her eyes.

6 Look at lines 162–185. Do you think Clare should wear red or not? Give reasons for your answer.

7 How does Clare use the glitter pens to help her?

8 Copy and complete the table to sum up the four stages of this story.

Stage of the story	Part of the story that matches this stage
Set-up	
Conflict	
Climax	
Resolution	

9 Find two places where you think the spoken narrative voice of this story is particularly effective. Explain why you chose your examples.

7 Planning your own short story

It is very easy to start a short story ... but sometimes quite difficult to end it. Often, writers plan to write only two or three pages and find they have written ten before they are anywhere near the resolution. The key is planning: knowing what kind of story you are going to write, what is going to happen, and to what kinds of characters.

Activity 1

1   In the Writing Activity on page 56, you are going to be asked to write a story about someone making a decision in his or her life. Think about:
    ● What kind of character might have to make interesting decisions?
    ● What might the decision be?
    ● Where would be the best place and time to set the story?

2   Plan the four key stages of your plot – **set-up**, **conflict**, **climax** and **resolution** – thinking about the different kinds of openings, developments and endings you have explored in this unit.

3   Even if you are happy with your plot idea, it's good to explore other ways in which you could structure your story. Look at this flow chart showing the plot of 'All That Glisters'.
    a   How would it affect the impact of the story if it had a different ending? For example:
        ● Clare refuses to do what her Aunt tells her.
        ● Clare asks her mother if she can change.
        ● Clare gives in completely and goes to the funeral dressed in her uniform.
    b   How would it affect the impact of the story if the structure of the story were different? For example, how would it change your response to the story if it began with (4) the day of the funeral and the rest of the story is told in flashback?

4   Think of two other ways of ending the short story you are planning. For each one, write a sentence or two, commenting on how this might affect your reader's response to the story.

1   Clare discovers glitter pens and wants to make something for her sick father.

2   She doesn't have enough money to buy the pens.

3   She manages to get the money by sacrificing lunch. It is too late – her father is dead.

4   Clare uses the pens to add colour on the day of the funeral. It is her way of remembering happiness with her father.

Activity 2

Now you have plotted the four key stages of your story, you need to focus on the development. Make a list of the three or four incidents that will build your story from the conflict to the climax.

Activity 3

1   Look at the work you did on characterisation on pages 36–39. Use a planning diagram like this to build up some of the details you could use to describe your main character.

2   When you describe a character, you do not need to give the reader every possible detail. Choose just three or four points from your planning which will give your reader a vivid picture of your character.

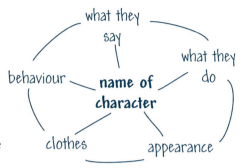

Activity 5

Look at this short story writer's checklist.

What other helpful advice would you add?

• You have done your planning – so stick to it!

• Don't just say what happened – use description to paint a picture in the reader's mind.

• Choose your vocabulary carefully, thinking about the effect it will have.

• Check your writing carefully as you go along and when you have finished.

Knowledge about language Overuse of pronouns

Pronouns are words that writers use to refer to a noun. Writers need to be careful they don't overuse pronouns and that it is clear which noun is being replaced.

Read the following paragraph.

> John and Alice met their friend Ben in the street. He asked them if they would like to go to the park to meet some other friends who were already there. She asked him if they were going to be there for long. He said that they would.

This paragraph contains too many pronouns. It isn't always clear who or what is being referred to. Change some of these pronouns so it is clear to the reader what is happening.

Writing Activity
Imaginative writing

Short stories: Decisions

You have been asked to write a short story for an anthology about someone making a decision in his or her life, and the consequences of that decision. This is the note you get from the publisher:

We are looking for complete short stories about making a decision – and the results of that decision.

Here are some guidelines:

Write in the first person – but you can write as yourself or as an imagined person. Try to create an individual style and voice for your character.

Decide whether the decision is important or trivial, whether your story is going to be humorous or serious, action-packed or reflective.

Think about the structure of your story. Are you going to start with the decision or with the consequences – or with some reflections on the experience?

Here are some possible openings, which you can use if you want to:

- It was a split-second decision. I knew almost immediately it was the wrong one ...

- The devastation was beyond description ...

- Thinking about it now, I don't know why at the time I thought it was such a good idea ...

- There are some experiences you would like to forget but somehow just can't ...

Your task

Write a short story about making a decision, for the anthology.

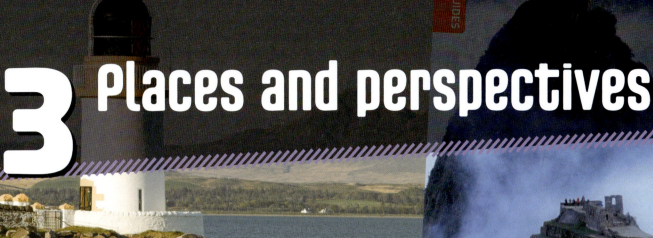

3 Places and perspectives

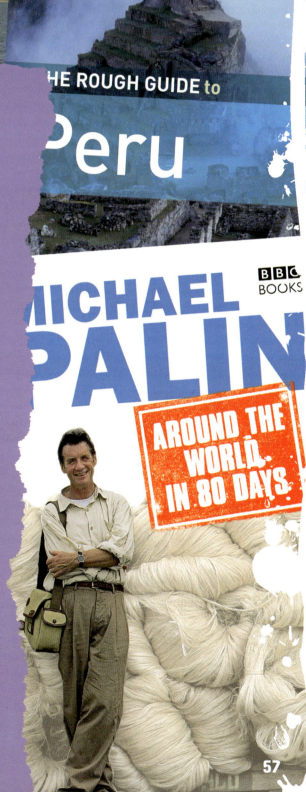

THE ROUGH GUIDE to

Peru

BBC BOOKS

MICHAEL PALIN

AROUND THE WORLD IN 80 DAYS

Experiences and outcomes

In this unit you will:

Reading
- read a range of texts about travel writing and recognise their different purposes
- comment on how writers' language choices create effect
- infer how a writer feels about a place, both implicitly and explicitly.

Writing
- plan pieces of writing to meet a specific purpose
- write a range of texts, including personal recount texts and texts to inform and guide
- use adjectives and adverbs to create effective descriptions of places.

Words and sentences
- use colons to link two parts of a sentence
- sequence sentences into the most logical order
- spell correctly, including the correct use of suffixes.

Talking and Listening
- work in groups to discuss and solve problems.

By the end of this unit you will:
- complete a piece of personal writing that reflects on an experience (Writing Activity: Personal and reflective writing)
- take part in a group discussion (Talking and Listening Activity: Group discussion).

1 What makes travel writing special?

You are learning:
- to understand the main features of travel writing.

Travel writing is always focused on a place, or the writer's experience of a place, other than home. The purpose of travel writing varies.
- Sometimes it is to **guide** others who might take a similar trip.
- Sometimes it is to **evaluate** a destination for possible visitors.
- On other occasions the purpose is to **share** an impression of a place or an interesting experience or journey.

Activity 1

Look at the following pieces of travel writing. Can you match them to the purposes described above?

Text 1

I arrived in Japan a dewy-eyed green sprout out of college, eager to devour a rich new culture and mingle with curious, exotic people. But after three months teaching in a smog-infested city near Tokyo, I was confronted mostly by other foreigners or garishly blonde Japanese bobbing their heads to Eminem, hypnotised by video games and fanatical about European labels. I couldn't help feeling that this wasn't the real Japan at all. Where was the land of the noble samurai, the whistling sakurabashis, the Zen harmony?

Text 2

Head back to the Jalan Raja, and veer left. You will come to the gleaming white Menara Dayabumi, with its fine filigree-like Islamic design. It is most impressive at night when its floodlit. Go past the general Post Office (open Mon–Fri 7.30a.m.–5p.m.) and take the pedestrian subway to the other side of Jalan Sultan Hishamuddin.

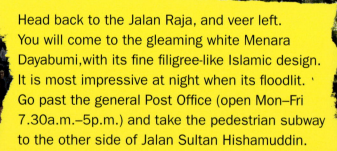

Text 3

If you're looking for the perfect way to have some serious fun and totally recharge, whatever the time of year, then look no further than Argyll – it's a winner. The range of accommodation will suit almost any purse and any group; from extended families on a budget to honeymooners with no financial limitations! It's got it all: good food, great views and activities galore. The only thing you can't guarantee is the weather!

Text 4

The sea became green, the rocks all grey, and then, as I watched, the rim of the sun rose over the horizon and the sea held it as a scimitar of fire. The white disc rose, a miracle; it looked very large, as if it had grown bigger in the night. It paused a moment in the sea and then suddenly seemed to bound up from it: it flooded the world with light.

Activity 2

Each of the different types of travel writing on page 58 is recognisable because of certain conventions, or special techniques, that the writers use.

1 Look at the list of writer's techniques below. Can you match them to the type of travel writing they are used in?

- emphasis on factual information such as opening hours
- use of descriptive detail
- matching of features of the place to the needs of travellers
- inclusion of map references and directions
- focus on positive aspects of the place
- discussion of positive and negative aspects of the place
- inclusion of web addresses and contact details
- focus on the writer's feelings and actions
- use of figurative language (words that paint pictures in your mind)
- use of comparatives (e.g. *bigger*) and superlatives (e.g. *most impressive*).

Use a table like the one below to record your ideas. The first technique has been inserted for you.

Type of travel writing	Writer's technique
Writing to guide	Use of comparatives and superlatives
Writing to evaluate	
Writing to share an experience	

2 Travel writers also structure their work differently depending on the reason why they are writing. For examples, read texts A–C.

Which structure best matches each type of travel writing in your table?

C

Each paragraph of my work concentrates on a specific aspect of a place, such as accommodation or things to see so that people can check out one thing at a time, or what's most important to them.

B

Usually my accounts have a chronological structure, although I do sometimes flash back or forward for effect.

A

I usually structure my writing so that my readers can walk or drive and read as they get to each place.

2 Writing to inform and guide

You are learning:
- to write clearly about a place so that a visitor could be guided by your instructions.

Common forms of travel writing include the guidebook and tourist information leaflet. They are written by 'experts' who either live in the country featured or have spent time getting to know it in order to pass on advice and tips. These types of guide are usually published as a book or an online resource. However, sometimes guides are written to lead visitors around a specific attraction and are only available once you get there.

Activity 1

1   Imagine you are planning a trip to a city that you have never visited before.

    Make a numbered list of all the questions you would find it useful to have answers to, in order to get the most out of your visit, such as:
    - How can I get around the city?
    - What sort of food is popular?

2   Now draw a timeline like the one below and place your questions on it, indicating when you would need to know the answer.

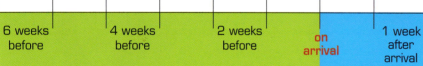

| 6 weeks before | 4 weeks before | 2 weeks before | on arrival | 1 week after arrival |

3   Look at the contents pages of the *Rough Guide to Iceland* below.

    Why do you think the author has ordered the information in each part in this way? Would you change the sequence they have used?

CONTENTS

Introduction ix

Activity 2

Sometimes guidebooks contain detailed instructions so that readers can navigate around an area or attraction.

1 Read the extract opposite from *The Insight Pocket Guide to the Seychelles* and make a list of the words that tell you what to do. Can you follow the route on the map?

2 Write a paragraph guiding readers to the Victoria market. Start your directions like this:

'You should start your walk facing the ...'

Test your instructions on a partner by getting them to trace the route on the map with their finger as you read it out to them.

Exit the gardens and turn left onto the main road and take the first turning off Le Chantier roundabout. This is Francis Rachel Street, which used to be the coastal road before the land to your right was reclaimed. The National Library is the big building to your right. Beyond it you will see the Cable and Wireless Building on the left. Look out for Kenwyn House, a traditional house owned by the company, set back from the road. A little further on the left, set well back, is Victoria's only mosque. Turn right just after this and park at the stadium car park.

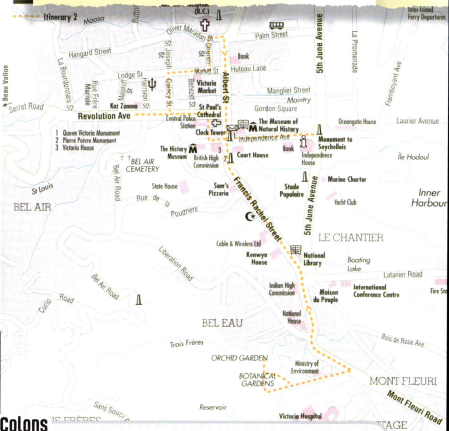

Knowledge about language Colons

Colons link two parts of a sentence. Writers of guidebooks often use colons because they can be used to signal that more information is coming.

Link the first and second parts of the sentences below so that they make sense.

The town is full of places to go	:	fashion capital, home of the Duomo and the Teatro alla Scala.
You won't be able to resist the centre	:	'It's the city that never sleeps.'
No wonder they say	:	it's full of things to do.
Milan	:	parks, museums, cafés and galleries.

3 Personal recount writing

You are learning:
- to recognise personal recount texts and write your own.

Recount texts focus more on explaining a sequence of events than on describing where they happened, or how they made the writer feel. However, many recount texts are only interesting because of the unusual nature of the people, places and events they describe.

Activity 1

Recount texts have a predictable structure. They begin by telling the reader *who* was involved, *what* happened and *where* and *when* this event took place. This is called the **orientation**.

1 Read this opening of a recollection by Catherine Jones. Information telling you who was involved in the story has been highlighted.

In my early twenties, nervous with anticipation, I arrive by ferry in Messina. I travel armed with a long list of relatives to visit on my first trip to Europe – a trip that will plant the seeds for the many years I will live abroad. My mother and her brother, first-generation Americans, have written well ahead, and I am told that my numerous Sicilian kin eagerly await my coming. Drawn by a sense of both familiarity and mystery, I too impatiently look forward to meeting the characters of the colourful tales with which my effusive great aunt has regaled me.

Captured in time, like a Victorian watercolour, the villa of my Uncle Ivan sits on a cliff overlooking the bay at the edge of the town. The concierge admits me through a gate in a high stone wall abutting the street, to a vista of tiered gardens which slope, exactly as I have seen in old family photos, toward the iridescent blue and enigmatic sea.

Inside the white villa, a blue tile motif echoes the Mediterranean which can be seen through floor-to-ceiling windows. Ivan's wife welcomes me tightly to her bosom, but Uncle Ivan is chilly and straight-backed. Their two young children scamper among aunts, uncles, cousins and curious neighbours.

2 Now complete a spider diagram like the one on the right.

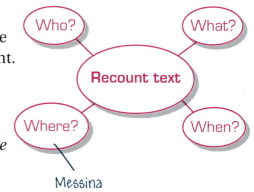

Activity 2

It is easy to recognise recount texts because they have a number of conventions:
- they focus on <u>individual people</u>, i.e. they use the words *I* or *we*
- they use words that indicate <u>when</u> (e.g. *before school*) and <u>where</u> the events took place (e.g. *outside the classroom*)
- they use words that <u>describe actions</u> (e.g. *helped, crushed*)
- they are nearly always written in the <u>past tense</u>.

Read this second extract from Catherine Jones' recollection. Does it follow the conventions listed on page 62? Record your evidence as a bulleted list under the four headings: 'Individual people', 'When/Where', 'Actions' and 'Past tense'. Words showing focus on individuals have been highlighted.

Uncle Ivan and his wife are dressed in their finest black silk. A current of excitement sparks the air. The day appears to promise some big event. Under the strict command of my uncle, maids scurry about, placing flowers, zipping dresses, making me feel uncomfortable. Could I please dress for the occasion? I am asked. We are leaving soon for a restaurant. I am tired from travelling and unprepared for such brouhaha, but dutifully comply as best as I can.

Seated at the restaurant with my relatives and a group of their friends, I am confronted with a long table laid with every possible extraction of the Mediterranean, shelled and unshelled morsels, many of which I cannot identify by name, but that taste heavenly. And this is only the first course of seven. Repeatedly, I seem to be compared to my mother's mother. At least I perceive this as relatives pinch my cheek and recite my grandmother's name.

Upon returning to the villa, I am escorted to my room to nap by a maid who points to an adjoining villa, newly built in the same style. Another maid whisks into the room, cradling a white formal gown in her arms like a newborn babe. She seems to beg my opinion. The dress is beautiful. I express what I feel is a fitting 'Aah!' for such a fine gown, which elicits a relieved sigh from the maid, a sigh as heavy and warm as the sirocco wind sweeping in from Africa.

Here is the surprise ending of Catherine Jones' story.

Back home in the Midwest, I am to find out from my cousins that I have missed a wedding and caused what might be a permanent family rift. The next-door villa pointed out by the maid was built for the bridal couple. The bridegroom was a young, handsome, Italian doctor from my uncle's university. And the bride? It was to have been my wedding – unbeknownst to me, prearranged by my Sicilian relatives, in accordance with their tradition. Often, I will wonder who this bridegroom was, and if we would have lived happily ever after …

Activity 3

Write your own recount text, using the three-part structure, giving an account of an incident that took place somewhere away from home, when something unexpected or embarrassing happened to you or a family member. Check that you have used all of the conventions, and an orientation and ending, as discussed in this unit.

4 Descriptions

You are learning:
● to understand how a writer uses images and adjectives to create a strong picture.

The purpose of some travel writing is to share the writer's impression of a place with the reader. The writer wants you to be able to imagine that you have been there too. To do this they often use language and comparisons that appeal to all five of your senses.

Activity 1

1 Read this description of Tortuguero National Park in Costa Rica.

Costa Rica

Tortuguero National Park can only be reached by boat or plane. There are no roads in and no roads out. The journey by boat is slow and sometimes laboured as the thick red mud sucks at the underside of the boat and fallen trees partially block the way, grasping at the passing craft with blackened fingers. Yet rapidly you are transported back in time and the jungle noises begin to hint at dinosaurs lurking within.

Loud braying calls and sudden startling shouts from Howler monkeys set the vast, looming, cliff-like walls of many greens, rustling and wavering. Like heads of fresh broccoli the tree canopies cluster together, competing for light. Strings of creeper hang spaghetti-ish from the huge trees they are slowly strangling: mad maypoles without dancers. Startlingly, sudden licks of flame cut through the green: blood-red Heliconias, white-hot Ibis wings and the electric-blue Morpho. At ground level the tree trunks are ringed by thick buttresses: black rockets ready to launch.

Tiny beaches of grey sand are littered with huge ribcages: long-fallen tree canopies now bleached and brittle waiting to be swept away in the next tide.

The river below you is like hot chocolate, or sometimes cold, ebony coffee in the shady inlets where nobbly Caymen lurk just under the surface, floating like logs. Green river turtles float tantalisingly close, 'E.T.' heads bobbing up and back down, disappearing in the murky depths.

2 Make a table like the one below. In the first column, select a word or phrase from the extract. In the second column, describe why you think the writer chose those particular words and phrases. Two have been done for you. Do at least another three.

Word or phrase	Explanation
no roads in and no roads out	This phrase explains that the park is remote and maybe dangerous.
hint at dinosaurs	The writer is suggesting that the landscape is ancient and mysterious.

Activity 2

Writers spend a lot of time choosing the words they will use so that all five of your senses are stimulated.

Draw a frame like the one on the right, then pick out 20 words from the extract and fit them into the correct area of the frame. Some words might fit into more than one category, in which case you can use the overlapping sections on the centre of the frame.

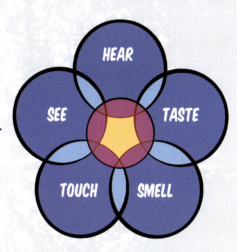

Activity 3

1 The writer compares the jungle scenery to several different things. Sometimes she uses similes:

'The river below you is like hot chocolate …'

'Strings of creeper hang spaghetti-ish'

and sometimes she uses a metaphorical sentence:

'… grasping at the passing craft with blackened fingers.'

Why do you think she chose these comparisons? Write down your ideas using the stem phrase:
'I think she chose this comparison because it makes me think about …'

2 Make up four more comparisons that could be inserted into sentences in the passage:
   a Create two similes (remember: a simile compares two things using *as* or *like*).
   b Next, create two metaphorical sentences (remember: a metaphor is where you say that one thing *is* another.)

Activity 4

A description of a place is not complete unless the writer has suggested what the mood of the place is like. This is called the **atmosphere**.

Sometimes a writer will give you very obvious information about the atmosphere of a place. At other times you have to read between the lines, or deduce the atmosphere of the place.

1 **a** Look at the annotations on this extract from the description of Tortuguero that you read on page 64.

   b Complete annotations 4, 5 and 6.

> 1 Not easy to get there …
> probably not many
> people … a lonely place.

> 2 It sounds like you'd be
> quite vulnerable as you
> couldn't escape fast …
> threatening place.

Tortuguero National Park can only be reached by boat or plane. There are no roads in and no roads out. The journey by boat is slow and sometimes laboured as the thick red mud sucks at the underside of the boat and fallen trees partially block the way, grasping at the passing craft with blackened fingers. Yet rapidly you are transported back in time and the jungle noises begin to hint at dinosaurs lurking within.

6

5

> 3 'Sucks' sounds as if the
> mud is alive and trying
> to eat the boat …
> scary … and weird

4

2 Which one of the statements below best describes the atmosphere created by the description of Tortuguero? Why?

'It is a lively, exciting place to be.'

'It is tense and exciting.'

'It is quite a threatening, mysterious place.'

'It is a boring, dull place.'

Activity 5

1 Look at the photographs on page 64 and the one opposite. They are all taken from a boat travelling through Tortuguero.

  a You are going to write a description of each picture. Decide what sort of atmosphere you want to create in your description.

  b Write one paragraph about each one, using as many adjectives and adverbs, comparisons and atmospheric details as you can to create a multi-sensory image for your reader.

Self-evaluation

Look at your descriptions of the photographs. Think about the words you have used. Which of these statements best fits your work?

Beginner	Competent	Expert
I chose a few of the words because I knew they would make my reader react	I chose most of the words because I knew they would make my reader react in a particular way	I was really careful to match the words I used with the effect I wanted to create

Knowledge about language Sequencing

1 An effective paragraph is one that contains sentences that are clearly grouped together for a reason. The writer of the description of Tortuguero (see page 64) decided to group her sentences by topic.

  Each of the headings below summarises the content of one of the paragraphs. Put them in the correct order to match the sequence used by the writer.

  A The beaches   C The water
  B The journey into the park   D The appearance of the trees

2 Look again at the second paragraph of the extract about Tortuguero. Why are the sentences placed in this order? Are they:

  a placed in chronological order
  b ordered to build up extra details and examples of an idea
  c sequenced to suggest the writer's eyes moving around the scene?

5 Author's point of view

You are learning:
- to analyse how writers use language to express a viewpoint, their ideas and emotions about a place or an experience.

Travel writing is often very personal. As you have seen, some types of travel writing are focused entirely on an individual's experience of a particular place or journey. Other people might have a totally different time there, and might feel very differently, even if they were doing the same things.

Activity 1

1 Read this extract from a story posted on a website called 'Tales from a small planet', written by ten-year-old Magdalena Travis.

File   Edit   View   Favorites   Tools   Help

Address http://www.talesmag.com   ☑ ➔ Go   Links »

 # Tales from a small planet

In the summer of 2004, my family moved to Accra, Ghana. I was seven years old then. On the one hand, I did not want to say goodbye to my friends in Poland where my family and I had been living – my Dad works for the U.S. State Department and Krakow was our first post. On the other hand, I was curious: what would Africa feel like? My image of Africa was a big sand dune with elephants, giraffes and zebras, covered with plantain trees and coconut palms.

Well, this was one of the times when I was wrong. Accra is a busy town with dusty winds from the Sahara during the harmattan season. Over the two years I spent here, a great number of exciting things happened. In Mole National Park, I saw elephants roaming free and naughty baboons stealing crackers and bananas. I learned to boogie board and enjoyed many days on sandy beaches finding sea shells and sand dollars. If I was thirsty, I'd ask my Mom for a drink and, as unreal as it seems, she would say: 'OK dear, why don't you find a man with a machete to climb up a tree and get a coconut for you?' Fresh coconut juice was my favourite drink in Ghana. One time I met a great Ashanti chief and danced at the festival in his village. I also had a great experience attending Lincoln Community School, an international school uniting many cultures.

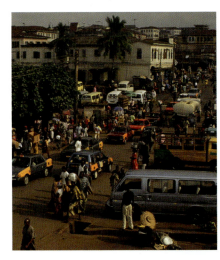

Normal days there were spent getting up at six-thirty, and then waiting for the bus to come between seven and seven-thirty. The bus would come at different times because of security concerns. I didn't like it, because you never knew if you'd be charging for the bus, or sleeping on it going home. Then we would go to school, eat a snack at nine, and eat lunch at twelve. We would come home on the bus (you were definitely not lucky if you were last to be dropped off!). On Saturdays and Sundays, my dad would pack us all in the car and we would be on our way to a beach. I would relax in the warm sand and then let the water carry me towards the waves on my boogie board. However, there is something you need to watch out for on a Ghanaian beach. It is the outdoor, behind-a-rock-or-straight-on-the-warm-sand OUTHOUSE! It can really stink up the place.

Once I met some village kids on the beach. I thought they wanted to play, and they did for a while, although they could hardly speak English and we had to find other ways to communicate. However, when my Mom called me for lunch and I was walking away, they begged me for money and food. I did not know what to do so I just ignored them, but it pretty much ruined my day. But then I started thinking ... Before I came to Ghana, I always thought everyone had the same amount of money. I soon came to learn that the world did not quite work in that way. This made my feelings mix and my stomach churn. I did not know quite what I was feeling. It was a mix of melancholy and fury. My mind was racing and for the first time in my life I realised that people were different not only by looks but by how much they had. Suddenly I thought the concept of money was not such a great idea after all. This feeling stayed with me for the rest of our tour in Ghana.

2 Sometimes writers are clear about their feelings about a place or experience; they even name them for us. Make a spider diagram like the one on the right, recording the emotions that Magdalena names in her piece of writing. You could add drawings or symbols to help you understand your notes later.

curious | How Magdalena felt | angry

3 The most effective pieces of writing usually present a clear reaction to a place. This helps to involve the reader, who usually wants to decide whether they agree or disagree. Magdalena's feelings at the start of her stay in Ghana are a little confused because she would rather not leave her friends, but once she settles down she clearly describes a consistent viewpoint about her new lifestyle.

a Complete a table like the one below showing her thoughts and feelings about Ghana. One example has been done for you. Add at least another three.

Positives	Negatives
Unusual animals to see	

b Would you say that Magdalena felt:
- more positive than negative
- more negative than positive
- a constant mixture of the two?

Activity 2

1 Another way in which writers give us clues about their viewpoint is by using words that have precise meanings. These words give us an idea of what and how strongly the writer is thinking and feeling. For instance, when Magdalena says: 'It can really stink up the place' (page 69) she could have used many other words instead of *stink*.

a Jot down at least five other words that describe a smell.

b Now put them into order, starting with the one that suggests the smell is bad and ending with a word that suggests the smell is good. Where does *stink* fit into your rank order?

2 Look at the extract opposite from Magdalena's story.

Think about the word *great*. Can you make a line of words that are similar in meaning and then use one in a sentence that would make your enjoyment seem even stronger than Magdalena's?

> I also had a great experience attending Lincoln Community School, an international school uniting many cultures.'

Activity 3

Writers can also make us guess how they are thinking and feeling about a place or experience. Sometimes we need to deduce or infer their ideas and emotions from the words and phrases they use. One way of doing this is to try to unpick all of the ideas a word puts into your mind. Imagine the word is like the tip of an iceberg and under the surface are all the ideas it puts in your head. Use these as clues to work out what the writer means.

a For instance, how do you think Magdalena was thinking and feeling when she wrote 'unreal as it seems' in paragraph 2 (page 68)?

b Now write a description of a place you really like, using some words that would give the reader a clear impression of your viewpoint. Use the writing frame below to order your thoughts.

_____ is a _____ place with so much to please.
Starting with the _____ a visitor is quickly _____ . Moving on to consider the _____ everyone is usually _____ by the _____ but if not then there's always the _____ to make you _____ .

Activity 4

The viewpoint of a travel writer can often be exaggerated. When a writer exaggerates for effect we call this **hyperbole**.

1   Read the extract below in which Alexander Smith writes about a journey made to the Cuillin mountains in Skye.

> Picking your steps carefully over huge boulder and slippery stone, you come upon the most savage scene of desolation in Britain. Conceive a large lake filled with dark green water, girt with torn and sharp precipices; the bases of which are strewn with ruin since an earthquake passed that way, and whose summits jag the sky with grisly splinter and peak. There is no motion here save the white vapour streaming from the abyss. The utter silence weighs like a burden on you; you feel like an intruder in the place. The hills seem to possess some secret; to brood over some unutterable idea which you can never know. You cannot feel comfortable at Loch Coruisk, and the discomfort arises in a great degree from the feeling that you are outside everything – that the thunder-splitten peaks have a life which you cannot intermeddle. The dumb monsters sadden and perplex. Standing there, you are impressed with the idea that the mountains are silent because they are listening so intently. And the mountains *are* listening, else why do they echo our voices in such a wonderful way?

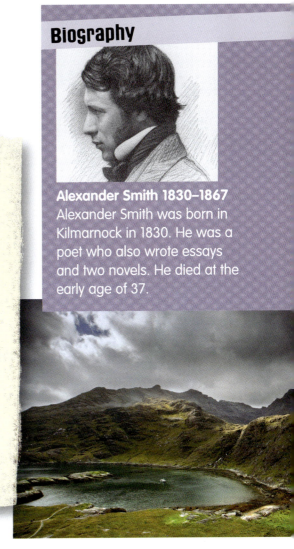

Biography

Alexander Smith 1830–1867
Alexander Smith was born in Kilmarnock in 1830. He was a poet who also wrote essays and two novels. He died at the early age of 37.

2   To what extent are the following statements true? Support your answers with quotations from the extract.

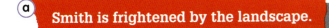

(a)   **Smith is frightened by the landscape.**

(b)   **Smith is impressed by what he sees.**

3   In this extract, the writer uses hyperbole. Find three examples of where his description of the landscape or his description of his feelings seems to be exaggerated.

Self-evaluation

The table below shows you how to get better at understanding a writer's point of view. How well are you doing?

Beginner	Competent	Expert
I can understand one simple idea or attitude clearly	I can understand more complex ideas	I can see how writers express their point of view in many ways

6 Creating two different views of the same place

You are learning:
- to compare the writing of two different authors.

Different travel writers often visit the same places. However, they do not always give the same picture of the place, or of what they have seen and done.

Activity 1

Read these two descriptions of travelling in Patagonia, a desert-like area of southern Argentina.

Extract A: from the diaries of Lady Florence Dixie

After another day's sojourn at this encampment we resumed our journey. We took a good supply of fuel with us, as we were now entering on the barren, woodless region, during our transit over which we should have to rely solely on the provision we now made.

Leaving the beechwood behind us we rode up on to a plain, on whose edge we could distinguish what appeared to be a little black cloud. In reality it was a peak, or rather clump of peaks of the Cordilleras, at the foot of which we were one day to camp, and towards which for the next few days we directed our horses' heads.

This day's ride, and it was a long one, was by far more monotonous and dreary than any of the preceding ones. The immense plateau over which we rode for six or seven hours was remarkable for its gloom and barrenness, even in a region where all is sterility and dreariness. There was no sun, and the sky, lowering and dark, formed a fit counterpart to the plain, which stretched flatly away to the indistinct horizon, grey, mournful, and silent.

We could not help being affected by the aspect of the scenery around us, and I do not remember ever to have felt anything to equal the depression of spirits to which I, in common with all our party, fell a prey, and to whose influence even the guides succumbed.

Extract B: from *Argentina*, a book of photographs by Florian von der Fecht

Nature is the main character in Patagonia, one of Argentina's most imposing scenes. Its rugged beauty always resisted attempts of conquerors and settlers who intended to control it in order to extend their power. Only those who persevered with extreme courage and determination were finally able to inhabit these desolate lands. With enormous personal sacrifice, some people settled in the valleys surrounded by arid plateaux where no drinking water was available; others chose to stay close to the coast, in barren lands with no vegetation and putting up with very tough, cold winters. And the wind … always the wind with its devastating ways. – 'Why then,' – Darwin wondered – 'do these arid lands possess my mind? Not only mine … I can't find a logical explanation but, in a way, I believe it may be because these lands widen the horizons of our imagination.'

Activity 2

Using the two extracts on page 72, copy and complete the table below with words or phrases that each writer uses to describe the different aspects of Patagonia.

	Extract A	Extract B
The size of the area		
The type of landscape		
The appearance of the land		
The amount of vegetation		
The amount of water		
The variety of experiences to be had		
The atmosphere		
The quality of light		
Colours featured		
Sounds heard		
The way people react to their surroundings		

Activity 3

1 Look at the list of statements below. Which ones express the viewpoint shown in extract A and which ones the viewpoint shown in extract B?

- Patagonia is boring.
- The landscape is impressive.
- Life in this region is difficult.
- There is not much to look at.
- The size of this area is a key point.
- The atmosphere is depressing.
- This area brings out the best in people.
- This area brings out the worst in people.
- The place is lifeless.
- This region stimulates the imagination.

2 Write a paragraph summing up how each writer feels about Patagonia. Use quotations to justify your opinions. Remember to explain how the words used affect your impressions.

Knowledge about language Suffixes

A suffix is a group of letters added onto the end of a word. Sometimes it is added to a word that already makes sense on its own, e.g: peace + ful = peaceful

At other times the root word has to change, e.g: happy+ly = happily

Complete these pairs of sentences describing two viewpoints on the same place, using the roots shown in brackets and one of the following suffixes:
-ion -ly -ant -ful -less -able -ing -ent

1 a Edinburgh is a (beauty) city full of (grace) buildings and (please) views.
   b Edinburgh is a (disgrace) place: full of (forget) views and (abhor) buildings.

2 a As I turned the corner my heart sank (rapid) and I realised it was (hope).
   b Every twist and turn of the path set my heart (pound) with (anticipate).

7 Writing a travel article for a newspaper or magazine

You are learning:
- to write a travel article to recommend or review a destination.

Most newspapers have a weekly travel section. This contains advertisements for holiday companies, hotels and resorts as well as a range of articles. Some of these are designed to offer recommendations to would-be travellers.

Activity 1

1   Read this article from *The Sunday Times*.

Instant weekend: Palma

There's more to the Mallorcan capital than playing sardines on a beach – such as fine eating, galleries and hotels, writes Chris West

Why should I go? This year, 9m people will fly to Mallorca. The good news is that 8,999,998 of them will head straight for the beaches, leaving you free to enjoy a compact collection of museums, galleries, restaurants and suave hotels.

What do I do? A stroll along the waterfront gives you the best view of La Seu Cathedral – a central landmark, with the old city arranged around and behind it. Built in the French-Gothic style, it's huge, with an altarpiece and giant candelabras by Gaudi. Es Baluard museum, home to modern photography, ceramics and paintings (www.esbaluard.org), is pretty spectacular to look at, too – it was created by adding stark concrete walls to the remains of Palma's 16th-century ramparts. It has an excellent restaurant, Es Robost d'Es Baluard serving new Mallorcan cuisine (9 Plaça Porta de Santa Catalina; 00 34-971 719609; £24pp). But if you're the kind of philistine (like me) who thinks that the best souvenirs come in 100% cashmere, make for Jaume III, one of the main shopping broadways. From there, go south, for the modern Spanish giants Zara and Massimo Dutti, as well as interesting little boutiques.

Where should I eat? Go straight to La Boveda, a noisy and authentic tapas bar on Carrer Boteria (971 714863). For those really in the know, there's Bar España, at the corner of Carrer del Bane and Calle de Can Escursac, farther up the hill into the old town (no telephone – and beware, they stop serving tapas at 10pm).

Where do I stay? If you're into posing in rooftop pools and flopping on four-poster day beds, try the Puro Hotel (www.purohotel.com; doubles from £173). It also has a private beach, a short taxi ride out of town, with massages and yoga (Cala Estancia, Can Pastilla; 971 744744). For true sanctuary, Hotel Convent de la Missio (www.conventdelamissio. com; doubles from £156) is a converted convent building in the old town, with a more ethereal vibe.

How do I get there? There are flights to Palma from 22 UK airports. Airlines include Jet2 (0871 226 1737, www.jet2.com), bmibaby (0871 224 0224, www.bmibaby.com), easyJet (www.easyjet.com) and Monarch (0870 040 5040, www.flymonarch. com). Aer Lingus (0818 365000, www. aerlingus.com) flies from Dublin.

Chris West travelled as a guest of the Spanish Tourist Office (020 7486 8077, www.tourspain.es).

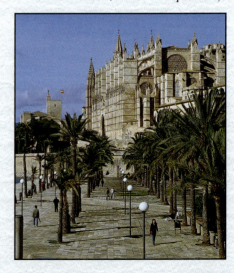

2 The writer of this article uses a number of strategies to recommend Palma to the readers. Can you find examples of the following techniques in the passage?

- using comparatives and superlatives
- matching attractions to specific types of visitor
- using words with positive associations.

Here are some examples taken from the early part of the article.
- Comparatives: 'There's more to the Mallorcan capital than…'
- Superlatives: 'the best souvenirs'
- Matching attractions to specific types of visitor:
  'The good news is that 8,999,998 of them will head straight for the beaches, leaving you free to enjoy …'
- Using words with positive associations:
  'compact collection of museums, galleries, restaurants, suave hotels.'

3 Imagine that your family wants to take a home-exchange holiday. Write a short article that could be used on a website to promote your home and its surroundings as a holiday destination. Start your entry:

> Welcome to your home away from home; it's got it all.
> For the comfort lover there is …

When you think you have finished, read it through and see if you can highlight examples of the three techniques that Chris West used opposite. If not, add some!

Knowledge about language Homophones

Homophones are words that sound the same but are spelt differently, e.g:
- there/their/they're
- new/knew
- your/you're
- heard/herd
- to/too/two
- past/passed

The best way to get them right is to learn what they mean and then work out which word fits where.

Proof-read this travel article and see how many homophone errors you can find. Be ready to explain why you think they are errors and to spell the word that should replace them.

I wasn't looking forward too my mid-week break in York, truth be told. It's chilly up their isn't it, and weather or not it rains is just a matter of time, I've herd. Someone at work had told me that York is big on Vikings, whatever that means! As soon as I arrived in the city I new I'd been wrong to wish myself sent elsewhere. The passed is everywhere you look: bits of ancient wall loom above you as you shop, Roman baths sit, empty and waiting, under your feet in the pub and ghosts lurk in every corner. Oh yes, and of course, the Vikings lie in wait two!

Writing Activity
Personal and reflective writing

Your experience

Your task

To write a piece of personal writing that aims to reflect on an experience you have had.

Throughout this unit you have seen that writing about places can have many different purposes and styles. Reflective writing tries to go beyond just telling the reader where you have been or what you have done. It attempts to reflect on the experience and it can do this in a variety of ways:

- it can explain how an experience has changed the writer
- it can reflect on how the place being visited is different from one which the writer knows better
- it can explain why a place is particularly important or notable
- it can reflect on the different culture of the people being visited
- it can explore how we can change the places that we visit.

1 Read this piece of writing by Robert Macfarlane. It describes how the summer visits to his grandparents' home inspired him to learn about mountaineering.

I was a 12-year-old in my grandparents' house in the Scottish Highlands when I first came across one of the great stories of mountaineering: *The Fight for Everest* – an account of the 1924 British Expedition during which George Mallory and Andrew Irvine disappeared near the summit of Everest.

We were staying in the house for the summer. My brother and I were allowed to go anywhere except into the room at the end of the hallway, which was my grandfather's study. […]

The best room in the house was the conservatory, which my grandparents called the Sun Room. Its floor was paved with grey flagstones, always cold underfoot, and two of its walls were giant windows. On one of the other windows my grandparents had stuck a black card cut-out in the shape of a hawk. It was supposed to scare away small birds but they regularly flew into the windows and killed themselves thinking the glass was air.

Even though it was summer, the inside of the house was filled with the cold mineral air of the Highlands, and every surface was always chilly to the touch. When we ate dinner, the chunky pieces of cutlery which came out of the dresser were cold in our hands. At night when we went to bed, the sheets were icy. I would wriggle as far down the bed as I could go, and hold the top sheet down over my head to create an airlock. Then I would breathe as deeply as I could until I had warmed up the bed.

There were books everywhere in the house. My grandfather had tried not to organise them and so very different books found themselves neighbours. […] There were several books about Russia whose titles I did not properly understand, and dozens about exploration and mountaineering.

One night, unable to sleep, I came downstairs for something to read. Against one side of the hallway was a long pile of books lying stacked on their sides. Almost at random, I pulled a big green volume out from halfway down the pile, like a brick from a wall, and carried it to the Sun Room. In the bright moonlight, I sat on one of the wide stone window-ledges and started to read *The Fight for Everest*. I already knew some of the details from my grandfather, who had told me the story of the expedition. But the book with its long descriptions, its 24 black-and-white photographs and its fold-out maps bearing unfamiliar place names – The Far East Rongbuk glacier, the Dzongpen of Shekar, The Lhakpa La – was far more potent than his account. As I read, I was carried out of myself and to the Himalaya. The images rushed over me. [...]

One passage of the book excited me more than any other. It was the description by Noel Odell, the expedition's geologist, of his last sighting of Mallory and Irvine:

> There was a sudden clearing of the atmosphere above me, and I saw the whole summit ridge and final peak of Everest unveiled. I noticed far away on a snow slope leading up to what seemed to me to be the last step but one from the base of the final pyramid, a tiny object moving and approaching the rock step. A second object followed, and then the first climbed to the top of the step. As I stood intently watching this dramatic appearance, the scene became enveloped in cloud …

Over and over I read that passage, and I wanted nothing more than to be one of those two tiny dots, fighting for survival in the thin air.

That was it – I was sold on adventure.

2 In what way would you say that this piece of writing is reflective? Use the bullet points on the previous page to help you.

3 Use an experience of your own to write your own reflective text. You do not need to have travelled far or gone to remote places to write a reflective text. A simple school day trip can give you enough to write about. The important thing is that you try to analyse the experience.

8 Organise a group presentation

You are learning:
- to work in groups to discuss and solve problems.

Doing anything in a group requires certain skills. Any decisions and actions will affect everyone. Does this mean that everyone has to have a say on every issue? How can disagreements be solved? What are the most important communication skills necessary for a good group discussion?

Activity 1

Read this transcript of an interview with 19-year-old student Luke Picknett about how he and his companions managed to work together to complete an exciting journey in the UK.

Interviewer: When you did the ten tors expedition on Dartmoor, was the group responsible for deciding the route that you would take and what you would pack?

Luke: We were told the ten tors that we were supposed to reach, then as a group of six we had to decide how we would actually get to them. We decided to divide up and take on certain roles. There was a leader and then two of us were in charge of navigation and then another two were in change of equipment and food. The leader had to make the final decision if we couldn't make up our minds.

Interviewer: Why do you think it was necessary to divide the work up like that?

Luke: Well, because it would have taken ages if we made all the decisions as a group of six. To be honest, some people don't really have a clue anyway, like, say, 'I can't cook so don't ask me what food to pack'! You have to give the right jobs to the right people.

Interviewer: Why do you think it would have been difficult if you had to confer with the whole group all of the time?

Luke: Because it would have caused arguments, it would have caused tensions, people would have had conflicting ideas and if you minimise that, it will make the whole expedition easier and the morale of the group better. But sometimes we did all discuss a decision – and then it's really important to listen to each other or you end up shouting! You also need to let everyone have their say, but not for too long, or people get stressy. At the end of the day the leader has to have the guts to say, 'That's it. I'm making a decision,' and everyone else has to live with it.

Imagine you are designing an advice leaflet, 'Top Tips to Success when Planning in a Group'. Pick out any useful tips from the interview above. In groups, choose a scribe (someone to record your ideas) and write the tips in a bulleted list, like the one that has been started for you below.
- Appoint a leader.
- Make a plan.

Activity 2

Now read this second extract, where Luke discusses another expedition, this time in Kenya. Use this extract to add your 'Top Tips' leaflet as a group.

Interviewer: There must be a lot of preparation for these trips and quite a bit of packing. How do you go about knowing what you need to take and making sure you've got the right things with you?

Luke: I made a list of the equipment I thought I would need. First of all I thought about the fact that I was going to a hot country, and divided all of my equipment down into categories, for example sleeping equipment and then clothing (which was quite difficult because I had to take clothing that would be relevant for a climb up a mountain but also for an equatorial climate, so I had to make sure that I packed shorts and thermals). I had to take into consideration the fact that I'd be carrying my stuff everywhere, so I tried to make it as lightweight as possible.

Interviewer: And did you ever take something that was totally inappropriate or see anybody with things that were just not right for the setting?

Luke: Well, one of the girls on the Kenya expedition took some hair tongs out with her, which was totally ridiculous. Obviously there's no electricity up a mountain – so she wouldn't be able to use those – ever.

Interviewer: So you've got to consider what the facilities are where you're going?

Luke: Yes, and the environment you're going to be living in and the things you'll be doing. That's really important so that you know what's appropriate to take with you.

Interviewer: You've done a lot of travelling, so how do you decide how you're going to get from A to B, or do you just always walk?

Luke: Definitely not, there is a public transport system in Kenya and it depends entirely on where you're going and how much time and money you've got. The most popular is a small mini-bus which seats 14 and they're very fast but they're also really dangerous, and then there are big coaches that are slightly more expensive. So, for example, when I was working for the charity, it was important to me to get round as cheaply as possible, so I would choose the option of the minibus despite the fact that it was dodgy.

Interviewer: Right, OK, but were there practical issues, like you couldn't take your luggage on a particular form of transport?

Luke: Yes, for example, on the minibuses it would be very uncomfortable – though it would be possible – to travel with all of your equipment, so you have to take that into account.

Self-evaluation

The table below shows you how to get better at listening and responding to others in a discussion. How well are you doing?

Beginner	Competent	Expert
I can see that it is important to listen and respond to what others say in a discussion	I can see that I should try to build on others' ideas and respond to them in a discussion	I can see that I need to be sensitive towards other group members and begin to try to evaluate their contributions

Talking and Listening Activity

Talking and Listening: Group discussion

Travel and tourism: good or bad?

Your task

In groups, decide whether travel and tourism has more advantages or disadvantages.

1 Read the following extracts about travel and tourism.

A

Twenty years from now you will be more disappointed by the things that you didn't do than by the ones you did do. So throw off the bowlines. Sail away from the safe harbour. Catch the trade winds in your sails. Explore. Dream. Discover.
Mark Twain

B

The world is a book and those who do not travel read only one page.
St Augustine

C

I can't think of anything that excites a greater sense of childlike wonder than to be in a country where you are ignorant of almost eveything.
Bill Bryson

D

Environmental damage often results from rapid and uncontrolled development due to tourism – the environment plays second best to tourism profits. All too often governments and private enterprises prefer to maintain their tourist economies rather than their ecosystems. As a result, tourism developments – often built in the most beautiful landscapes and places in the world – threaten and destroy environments and exhaust limited natural resources, destroying these places for local peoples and future tourists.

Waste created by the tourism industry is difficult to remove from fragile areas and means mountains of rubbish are appearing in the most beautiful landscapes on earth.

E

One study estimated that a single transatlantic return flight emits almost half the CO_2 emissions produced by all other sources (lighting, heating, car use, etc.) consumed by an average person yearly.

F

Tourism is important to Scotland as:
- spending by tourists in Scotland amounts to over £4bn annually
- this spending supports around 200,000 jobs
- a disproportionate number of these jobs are located in rural areas where employment opportunities are limited.

G

H

CELEBRATE SCOTLAND.

The Callanish Standing Stones, Lewis, Outer Hebrides

Autumn is the perfect time to celebrate Scotland in all its glory, with fantastic golfing and fishing, woodland walks through golden forests, and the glens echoing to the roar of rutting stags. The cities are vibrant and buzzing with shows, exhibitions and world-class restaurants serving up the season's bountiful harvest. And the excitement is already building for next year's Homecoming Scotland festivities. For details of offers which make Scotland even more attractive than ever, click on visitscotland.com/celebrate.

Live it. Visit *Scotland.*
visitscotland.com/celebrate
0845 22 55 121

2 a In your groups, complete the table below. Choose one person in the group to be a scribe (someone who writes down the ideas of the group). Decide whether each item is making positive or negative comments about travel and tourism and express in your own words what it is saying.

Extract	Positive	Negative
A		

b Draw conclusions. Does your group think that the advantages of travel and tourism outweigh the disadvantages? Be prepared to justify your answer and report back. You can use any other materials from this unit or your own knowledge and research to back up your point of view.

Peer-evaluation

Now you need to decide how well you worked as a group and as individuals within that group. You have to decide on a set of criteria by which to judge everyone in the team. Make a list of the skills and qualities that were useful in this assessment task. For example:

- listened to other people's ideas
- made useful suggestions.

Make a table like the one below, writing these criteria as headings along the top of the table and the names of your group members down the first column.

	Took a role and stuck with it	Made useful suggestions	Listened to other people	Encouraged other people to make suggestions
Jo				
David				

Next, ask yourself whether you showed those skills and qualities during this task. Give yourself a rating from 1 (a little) to 3 (a lot). Ask everyone in the group to rate you, so that you get a realistic overview of your contribution.

4 The language of warfare

Experiences and outcomes

In this unit you will:

Reading
- recognise links between ideas, themes or characters
- support points with precise evidence and explanation
- analyse in depth and detail writers' use of literary, rhetorical and grammatical features and their effects
- explore how the meaning of texts is affected by how they are structured and organised.

Writing
- choose words carefully, considering how your choices will create precise or more subtle meanings according to task, purpose and reader
- control the response of readers, by using specific linguistic and literary techniques for deliberate effect.

Talking and Listening
- analyse the underlying themes or issues in spoken texts, identifying implied and explicit meanings.

Words and sentences
- use noun phrases to improve your descriptive writing
- identify modal verbs and understand their effect
- use semi-colons to link statements.

By the end of this unit you will:
- explore and comment on two poems (Reading Activity: Analysis of two poems)
- explore and comment on a persuasive speech (Talking and Listening Activity: Listening and responding).

1 Describing war

People have been writing about and describing wars for hundreds of years. The way a writer writes about war affects how we – the readers – feel about it. One description of a battle might emphasise danger, fear and horror; another might emphasise action and excitement. Before you read how some writers have described battles, think about how *you* would feel about war.

Activity 1

Imagine that *you* are fighting in a battle.

1 Write down words to describe how you feel during the battle.

2 Write down a list of words to describe the atmosphere or mood of the battlefield, e.g. *frightening, noisy, confused.*

3 Compare your words with someone else's.

Activity 2

1 Read this extract from *Strange Meeting* by Susan Hill. A man called Hilliard is going into battle during the First World War (1914–1918).

> As the noise of the artillery got louder his excitement seemed to fill his body, took him over entirely so that, when they themselves began to go up and over the top, he was no longer conscious of anything except the urge
> 5 to move forward, to keep up this almost hysterical sense of pleasure in what was so obviously a perfect battle, so easy, effortless. He felt as though he were standing outside himself, and was surprised at this new person he had become, surprised at everything. He wondered
> 10 when he would come to.

Biography

Susan Hill 1942–
Susan Hill was born in Scarborough in England. In a long and successful career she has written many novels for adults and young people. Probably her most famous novel is the ghost story, *The Woman in Black*. She borrowed the title *Strange Meeting* from a poem about the First World War by Wilfred Owen.

2 Copy and complete the table below to explore Hilliard's feelings.

Detail	What it suggests Hilliard is feeling
'excitement seemed to fill his body'	At first the only thing he seems to feel is excitement: it seems to have taken him over completely …
'the urge to move forward'	
'almost hysterical sense of pleasure'	
'He felt as though he were standing outside himself'	

3 Continue reading this text. Notice how Hilliard's feelings change as the battle goes on.

Where the ground began to slope up, the mud gave way to grass here and there. But they could no longer see the men on the right and left flanks because of the denseness of the smoke. Hilliard was separated from ₁₅ Barton and not so far ahead, so that when the rifle and machine gun fire opened up from the enemy guns hidden in Barmelle Wood, he had a better view. He watched their own first line stagger and fall, the men going ₂₀ down one after another on their knees and then, before the smoke closed up, the line immediately behind. It went on like that and after a moment they themselves were caught up in it, and the heavy shells began to come ₂₅ over, the whole division was an open target for the enemy guns. Wave after wave of men came walking into the fire, the ground began to open under their feet, as the **howitzers** blew up dozens of men at a time. ₃₀

Hilliard began to try and pull his own section of the line together. As the men fell he began shouting at them to close in, before an attack of coughing from the smoke and fumes forced him to stop, gasping for breath. Four ₃₅ men ahead of him and O'Connor on his right went down in the same burst of machine gun fire and he wondered how it had missed him so neatly. He went on.

After that he lost touch, the men coming up ₄₀ behind overtook his own section and fell in the same places, so that the bodies were piling on top of one another, the shell holes were filled and then new ones opened up, filled again. Once, Hilliard slipped and fell and for ₄₅ a moment thought that he had been hit, but could feel no pain. A Corporal beside him was holding his head between his hands, covering his eyes and rocking silently to and fro. Hilliard crawled over, hunted for his ₅₀ water bottle and got a little of it between the man's lips, but as it dribbled down his throat, he coughed it up with a great spout of blood, and his head fell forwards. Hilliard left him, got up again. He had no idea how far he had ₅₅ gone, he could see nothing. He thought they had begun to walk into their own artillery barrage, but there was a constant spray of fire from the enemy line. He had a clear picture of the whole army caught in the neatest, ₆₀ simplest possible trap. Another line of men came up the slope. A **Company**, he thought, stepping between the already dead and wounded, walking directly on into the rain of fire, and suddenly, Hilliard wanted to stand ₆₅ up and wave at them, shout, push them back, he saw that it was all useless, that those few who did reach the enemy line would be shot to pieces on their **wire**. He turned and began to roar at the first man who came towards ₇₀ him but before he was near enough he fell forwards, his knees giving slowly under him and his helmet slipping over his face.

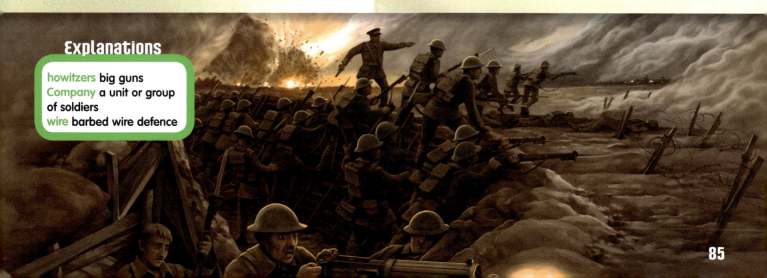

Explanations

howitzers big guns
Company a unit or group of soldiers
wire barbed wire defence

4 How do Hilliard's feelings change as the battle goes on? Explain your views carefully and refer to details in the text to support them.

Activity 3

Strange Meeting is a fictional account of a real war. The battle description you are about to read is very different: it comes from the science fiction novel, *The War of the Worlds*, in which Martians invade the Earth.

1 Read this account of the battle and think about the sort of atmosphere the writer, H.G. Wells, is trying to build.

The fighting was beginning. Then suddenly we saw a rush of smoke far away up the river, a puff of smoke that jerked up into the air and hung, and **forthwith** the ground heaved under foot and a heavy explosion shook the air, smashing two or
5 three windows in the houses near, and leaving us astonished.

Quickly, one after the other, one, two, three, four of the armoured **Martians** appeared, far away over the little trees, across the flat meadows that stretched towards Chertsey, and striding hurriedly towards the river.

10 Then, advancing **obliquely** towards us, came a fifth. Their armoured bodies glittered in the sun as they swept swiftly forward upon the guns, growing rapidly larger as they drew nearer. One on the extreme left flourished a huge case high in the air, and the ghostly, terrible **Heat-Ray** I had already seen
15 on Friday night smote towards Chertsey, and struck the town.

At sight of these strange, swift, and terrible creatures the crowd along by the water's edge seemed to me to be for a moment horror-struck. There was no screaming or shouting, but a silence. Then a hoarse murmur and a movement of feet
20 – splashing from the water. I turned, too, with the rush of the people, but I was not too terrified for thought. The terrible Heat-Ray was in my mind. To get under water! That was it!

'Get under water!' I shouted, unheeded.

I faced about again, and rushed towards the approaching
25 Martian – rushed right down the gravelly beach and headlong into the water. Others did the same. The stones under my feet were muddy and slippery, and the river was so low that I ran perhaps twenty feet scarcely waist-deep. Then, as the Martian towered overhead scarcely a couple of hundred
30 yards away, I flung myself forward under the surface.

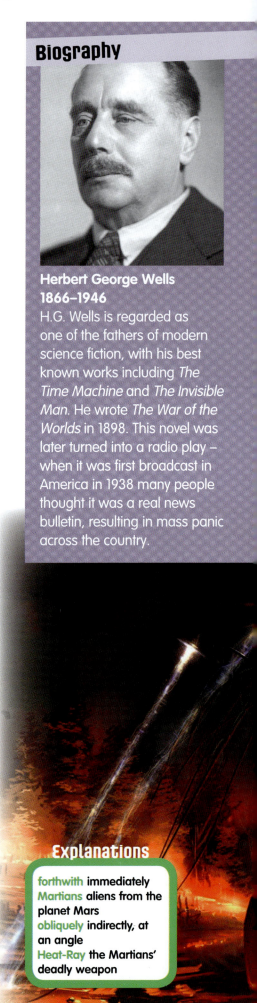

Biography

Herbert George Wells 1866–1946
H.G. Wells is regarded as one of the fathers of modern science fiction, with his best known works including *The Time Machine* and *The Invisible Man*. He wrote *The War of the Worlds* in 1898. This novel was later turned into a radio play – when it was first broadcast in America in 1938 many people thought it was a real news bulletin, resulting in mass panic across the country.

Explanations

forthwith immediately
Martians aliens from the planet Mars
obliquely indirectly, at an angle
Heat-Ray the Martians' deadly weapon

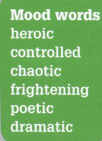

2 Look at the list of 'mood' words.
   a Which one of these words best describes the mood or atmosphere of Wells' battle writing?
   b Can you think of another word that better describes the mood?

3 Look at these quotations from *The War of the Worlds* extract.
   a 'the ground heaved under foot'
   b 'strange, swift, and terrible creatures'
   Explain what sort of atmosphere each of these quotations helps to create.

4 **a** Choose two other phrases or words from the passage on page 86 that help to create the mood or atmosphere of the battle. You could choose from:
   ● 'armoured bodies glittered in the sun' (line 11)
   ● 'horror-struck' (line 18)
   ● a word or phrase of your own choice.
   b Explain how the writer's choice of each word or phrase contributes to the mood or atmosphere of the description.

> **Mood words**
> heroic
> controlled
> chaotic
> frightening
> poetic
> dramatic

Activity 4

Go back to the notes you made on page 84 about your imagined battle. Using your notes and ideas from the battle descriptions in *The War of the Worlds* and *Strange Meeting,* write your own battle description. Write in the first person ('I…') as though you were actually there.

Sharpen your skills Noun phrases

A phrase is more than one word, but less than a whole sentence: *a fierce struggle*, for example. A noun phrase is an easy way of giving more information about something: e.g. not just a struggle, but a *fierce* one. A fierce struggle *for power* would extend the noun phrase a bit further. Here are some other examples of extended noun phrases:
a her large <u>bunch</u> of beautiful flowers…
b the long, slow <u>journey</u> south…
c the greatest surprise of all…
d the only way out…

1 Each noun phrase has a 'headword' which the rest of the phrase supports. In a and b above the headword is underlined. What is the headword in c and d?

2 Using noun phrases to add detail is a simple and effective way to improve your descriptive writing. Write a short phrase around each of the following noun headwords.
   ● house   ● picture   ● happiness

3 Write down three good examples of noun phrases from *The War of the Worlds* text on page 86. Explain how these noun phrases make effective descriptive phrases.

87

2 War prose

You are learning:
- to interpret a piece of prose fiction and appreciate how meanings are conveyed.

Remembrance by Theresa Breslin is an award-winning novel published in 2002. It explores the First World War and its impact on the lives of young people from a Scottish village.

Biography

Theresa Breslin
Theresa Breslin is a librarian and writer whose children's books have won many awards. She was born and brought up in Scotland and her writing covers many genres from real-life to science fiction.

Activity 1

Read the extract from *Remembrance*. In this extract, Alex reflects on his experience in a major battle.

Alex knew that the main reason he had survived the battle zone around Ypres was Corporal Eric Kidd. The older man had minded him ever since they had arrived at the Front. And Alex also knew that it was more than just his life that Eric was concerned about. The corporal was troubled by Alex's reasons for joining up.

'Revenge sorts nothing, son,' he said, when Alex eventually told him why he had enlisted. 'Your brother is dead. If you kill all the Germans in the world, he'll still be dead. Get revenge out of your head, and make room for your heart to grieve.'

On the journey down to the southern part of the line the men talked of their part in the ongoing action in what the officers were calling the third battle of Ypres. Alex had always imagined that being in a battle would be a definite thing. Commanders would lead at the front, and everyone would know exactly what was happening. He had thought almost that he would be able to watch the action as well as take part. He had not envisaged the mess, the chaos, the running and shouting, the unbearable noise, and the overwhelming awfulness of it. He had been part of the great push that was still going on, and had no clear awareness of what was actually happening. It was his first experience of an attack and he had hated everything about it. There was no excitement, no joy of marching forward together to defeat the enemy, only a dull tense pain of dreadful anticipation in his gut and then an explosion of gunfire and confusion. On his first engagement a man had fallen and died right in front of him, and when Alex had stopped and bent over to see if he needed help, Eric had grabbed him by the collar and dragged him away.

'Stretcher-bearers will get him, son.'

'No they won't,' said Alex. The truth of what he had said sinking into his consciousness as he spoke. Throughout the fighting the bodies just lay there and eventually decomposed or disappeared into the mud.

There were newspaper reports which the men talked about. People were saying that 'their boys' were beginning to win through. Alex had no idea of what ground they had gained. If anyone had asked him where he had fought, he would not have known.

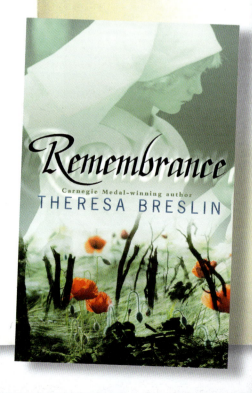

Activity 2

1 Men joined the army for many different reasons. Why had Alex enlisted in the Army?

2 **a** What had Alex expected war to be like? Where might he have taken this view from?

   b How does Alex's experience of war differ from what he had expected it to be? Pick out some words and phrases as evidence.

3 Find some evidence from the passage to suggest that Corporal Kidd is kind. Does his treatment of the dead man surprise you?

4 **Register** is a term used to describe words and phrases associated with a particular situation or subject matter. Pick out the words and phrases used by Theresa Breslin which you feel belong to the register of war. How does using the register of war create the right mood?

5 At the end of the extract there are some comments about newspapers.
   a Explain in your own words what the newspapers are saying.
   b How truthful do you think these news reports are? Justify your answer.

Activity 3

Write Alex's diary extract for that day. In your diary extract think about:
- what events would stick in his mind
- how he feels about his experience of war
- how he might describe events in a diary that only he would read.

You could use the sentence starters below to help you, or think of your own.

- Today has been very upsetting ...
- I learned that war was nothing like I thought ...
- I will never forget what happened as long as I live ...
- I owe a great debt to Corporal Kidd ...

3 War songs

You are learning:

● to interpret the lyrics of a war song and appreciate how meanings are conveyed.

War has inspired some very powerful poems and songs. Some of these are about the glory of dying for your country; others are about the horror of warfare. 'Logan Braes' by Robert Burns has a clear message about war. Burns put these words to an existing tune – called 'Logan Water' – in 1793. 'Logan Braes' was not published until several years after Burns' death because of its controversial views.

Activity 1

Read this extract from the lyrics to 'Logan Braes'.

> O Logan, sweetly didst thou glide,
> That day I was my Willie's bride,
> And years **sin syne** hae o'er us run,
> Like Logan to the simmer sun:
> 5 But now thy flowery banks appear
> Like drumlie winter, dark and drear,
> While my dear lad maun face his **faes**,
> Far, far frae me and Logan braes.
>
> Again the merry month of May
> 10 Has made our hills and valleys gay;
> The birds rejoice in leafy bowers,
> The bees hum round the breathing flowers;
> Blythe Morning lifts his rosy eye,
> And Evening's tears are tears o' joy:
> 15 My soul, delightless a' surveys,
> While Willie's far frae Logan braes.
>
> Within yon milk-white hawthorn bush,
> Amang her nestlings sits the thrush:
> Her faithfu' mate will share her toil,
> 20 Or wi' his song her cares beguile;
> But I wi' my sweet nurslings here,
> Nae mate to help, nae mate to cheer,
> Pass widow'd nights and joyless days,
> While Willie's far frae Logan braes.
>
> 25 O **wae** upon you, Men o' State,
> That brethren rouse to deadly hate!
> As ye make monie a fond heart mourn,
> Sae may it on your heads return!
> Ye mindna 'mid your cruel joys
> 30 The widow's tear, the orphan's cry?
> But soon may peace bring happy days,
> And Willie hame to Logan braes!

Biography

Robert Burns 1759–1796
Robert Burns was born in Alloway, Ayrshire. He came from a very humble background and achieved national fame in his life for his writing. In a short life of 37 years, he produced hundreds of memorable poems and songs about a whole range of topics. His poems and songs are still popular worldwide and his birthday (25 January) is celebrated at Burns Suppers where his works are performed, his life discussed and traditional Scottish foods are eaten. For many people, Burns represents Scotland and what it is to be Scottish.

Explanations

sin syne since then
faes enemies
wae sorrow

Activity 2

In this song, Robert Burns uses the technique of adopting a persona. This is when the poet writes from someone else's point of view.

1   Who is the speaker in this song? Why has Burns chosen this persona?

2   How do you think the narrator feels about this place? Pick out the words and phrases that show us this.

3   There is a strong contrast between how the narrator felt in the past and how she is feeling now, in the present.
    a   Which words describe her feelings in the present?
    b   What mood is created by these words?

4   Look again at the third verse. How does the narrator use the image of a thrush to show how she is feeling?

Activity 3

1   In the final verse the narrator gives her opinions about war and those who start wars.
    a   Who does the narrator mention?
    b   What effect does she say that war has on ordinary people?
    c   What does she hope will happen to those who start wars?

2   Look again at the last two lines of the song. What mood does the song finish on?

Self-evaluation

Look back at your work from Activities 1–3. Decide how well you are working and what you need to do to improve.

Beginner	Competent	Expert
I can clearly identify the writer's overall purpose and feelings	I can clearly identify the writer's main purposes and feelings	I am beginning to develop an analysis of the writer's purpose
I can show awareness of the general effect of the text on the reader	I can back up and develop views by referring to details in the text	I am beginning to develop an analysis of how the writer's viewpoint is built throughout a text
I can give some explanation of *how* the writer conveys his or her feelings	I can explain clearly *how* the writer conveys his or her feelings	I can explore *how* particular techniques affect the reader

4 Comparing poems

You are learning:
- to compare ideas in poems with a similar theme.

Often war poems deal with the loss of life on a very personal level. Poets do this in various ways to create different effects. Ewart Alan Mackintosh and Sydney Goodsir Smith both wrote poems considering the effect of death on the families of soldiers.

Activity 1

1 Read 'In Memoriam' by Ewart Alan Mackintosh.

So you were David's father,
And he was your only son,
And the new-cut peats are rotting
And the work is left undone,
5 Because of an old man weeping,
Just an old man in pain,
For David, his son David,
That will not come again.

Oh, the letters he wrote you,
10 And I can see them still,
Not a word of the fighting,
But just the sheep on the hill
And how you should get the crops in
Ere the year get stormier,
15 And the **Bosches** have got his body,
And I was his officer.

You were only David's father,
But I had fifty sons
When we went up in the evening
20 Under the arch of the guns,

And we came back at twilight –
O God! I heard them call
To me for help and pity
That could not help at all.

25 Oh, never will I forget you,
My men that trusted me,
More my sons than your fathers',
For they could only see
The little helpless babies
30 And the young men in their pride.
They could not see you dying,
And hold you while you died.

Happy and young and gallant,
They saw their first-born go,
35 But not the strong limbs broken
And the beautiful men brought low,
The piteous writhing bodies,
They screamed 'Don't leave me, sir',
For they were only your fathers
40 But I was your officer.

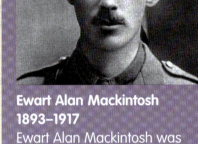

Biography

Ewart Alan Mackintosh 1893–1917
Ewart Alan Mackintosh was an officer of the 5th Battalion Seaforth Highlanders. He wrote 'In Memoriam' after an incident on 16 May 1916, when he attempted to carry the wounded Private David Sutherland to safety following an attack on the German trenches. Private Sutherland died and Mackintosh had to leave his body before returning to the British lines. He was awarded the Military Cross for his actions that day. Mackintosh was killed on 21 November 1917. He was 24 years old.

Explanation

> **Borches** Germany

2 Whose viewpoint is the poem from?

3 Look at lines 9–12. What is the speaker suggesting by these lines?

4 Now look again at the final verse (lines 33–40).
   a What contrasting images of the soldiers are created?
   b What does this contrast suggest about the speaker's experience of war and his feelings towards his soldiers?

5 In line 27, the speaker refers to the soldiers as 'More my sons than your fathers'.' What does this suggest?

Activity 2

The next poem describes a mother's grief at her son being killed in war. It was published in 1946.

1 Read 'The Mither's Lament' by Sydney Goodsir Smith.

> What care I for the leagues o sand,
> The prisoners and the gear they've won?
> My darling **liggs** amang the dunes
> Wi mony a mither's son.
>
> 5 Doutless he deed for Scotland's life;
> Doutless the statesmen dinna lee;
> But och tis sair **begrutten** pride
> And wersh the wine o victorie!

Explanations

liggs lies
begrutten tear stained

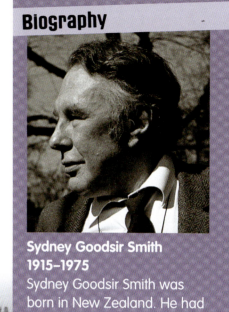

Biography

**Sydney Goodsir Smith
1915–1975**
Sydney Goodsir Smith was born in New Zealand. He had a Scottish mother and writing in Scots was important to him. He studied at Oxford and Edinburgh universities.

2 a Why do you think the poem opens with a rhetorical question?
   b What does this show about how the mother is feeling about the loss of her son?

3 What effect does the repetition of 'doutless' (doubtless) create at the start of the second verse?

4 The word 'wersh' is a Scots adjective used to describe anything bitter tasting. Explain how this helps to create the tone at the end of the poem.

Activity 3

Both poems deal with the theme of loss in war. Make a table, like the one below, comparing the similarities and differences in how the two poems deal with this theme.

	'In Memoriam'	'The Mither's Lament'
Speaker		
Subject of the poem		
Use of Scots		
Tone		

5 Structure in poetry

You are learning:
● to understand how a writer structures phrases and sentences for impact.

We have already seen how descriptions of war often use language to create particular effects. During the First World War (1914–1918), posters were carefully designed so that their words and images would have an impact on the public and persuade them to support the war effort.

Activity 1

Explain how each poster tries to persuade men to join the army. Refer to details in the posters.

Activity 2

The writer of the poem 'Futility', Wilfred Owen, imagines that the warmth of the sun might bring a dead soldier back to life – just as it used to wake him when he was at home on his farm.

A

Daddy, what did YOU do in the Great War?

B

YOUR KING & COUNTRY NEED YOU

TO MAINTAIN THE HONOUR AND GLORY
OF THE
BRITISH EMPIRE

1 Read versions A and B of the first verse of 'Futility'. One of them is by Owen and the other was written based on one of his early drafts.

Version A, verse 1

Drag him into the sun –
Gently its touch awoke his trance,
At home, whispering of fields not done.
Always it woke him, even in France,
5 Until this morning and this snow.
If anything might get him to go
The good old sun will know.

Version B, verse 1

Move him into the sun –
Gently its touch awoke him once,
At home, whispering of fields unsown.
Always it woke him, even in France,
5 Until this morning and this snow.
If anything might rouse him now
The kind old sun will know.

Biography

Wilfred Owen (1893–1918)
Wilfred Owen fought in the First World War as an officer. He wrote many well-known poems about his experience of war. In 1917, after suffering from shellshock, he was taken into the military hospital at Craiglockhart, Edinburgh. There he developed his skills as a poet and met other major writers of the time. He recovered and rejoined the war. Owen won the Military Cross for bravery, but was killed in action just seven days before the end of the war.

2 Make a list of the main differences between versions A and B. Look carefully at the ends of the lines.

3 Choose two of the differences. For each one, say which you prefer and give your reasons.

4 Now read verse 2 (the final verse) of the poem.

Verse 2

Think how it wakes the seeds, –
Woke, once, the clays of a cold star.
10 Are limbs, so dear-achieved, are sides,
Full-nerved, – still warm, – too hard to stir?
Was it for this the clay grew tall?
– O what made **fatuous** sunbeams toil
To break earth's sleep at all?

Explanation

fatuous idiotic, pointless

a What do you think the poet means when he asks: 'Was it for this the clay grew tall?'

b What point is the poet making about dying in battle?

5 What clues does the structure of verse 2 give you about which version of verse 1 the poet actually published?

Activity 3

Imagine you are a publisher. Wilfred Owen has sent you versions A and B of verse 1, and asked you to choose which one to publish. Here is part of his letter to you.

```
and I would like readers to feel moved
by my poem. I would like it to make them
think about the sadness of death in war.
To help them do that I have been trying to
write the poem so that it is slow, sad and
full of dignity, so that it has the sort
of tone that would make it suitable to be
read out at the soldier's funeral...
```

Write a reply to Owen telling him which version you will publish. Give him full reasons for your decision.

Reading Activity
Analysis of two poems

'We Shall Remember Them' and 'For a Dead African'

Your task

The two poems that follow are both about war. Read each one, then complete the activities that follow. The first is written by Sheila Parry and the second Dennis Brutus.

'We Shall Remember Them' was written after the Falklands Conflict, a war between Argentina and the UK which took place March–June 1982. The conflict was about which country 'owned' the Falkland Islands, South Georgia and the South Sandwich Islands. More than 900 lives were lost, including 255 members of the British armed forces, but the war sparked a wave of patriotism and did much to boost the popularity of the government at the time.

We Shall Remember Them

No visit to a gracious Queen,
No presentation honouring the dead.

The day his medal came
Her fingers fumbled with the padded envelope;
5 Ribbon and steel dropped from her hand,
Another piece rolled out of sight.

When they came home they found her there,
Tears falling on the polished floor
Trying to fit the fragments of her son,
10 To make sense of the scattered jigsaw of his life.

Home-assembly decoration kits
By order of a grateful government,
Broken like the bodies
They were made to celebrate.

15 But then he was, at seventeen, hardly a soldier.
Just a name and number in the power game.
Mail-order hero of a battle scene.

1 a What does the title 'We Shall Remember Them' suggest the poem is going to be about?
  b How do the first two lines create a different impression from the title?

2 'Her fingers fumbled with the padded envelope' (line 4)
  What impression do you get of the mother from this line of the poem?

3 a How does the poet use the image of the broken jigsaw (verse 3) to describe both the medal and the son's life?
  b 'Home-assembly decoration kits' (line 11)
  What does the choice of language in this quotation suggest about the medal?

4 In the final verse (lines 15–17), how does the poet indicate that the young man who has died was regarded as unimportant?

5 a Read the following statements about the poem.

Statement 1: The young man was very brave to go and fight in the army and we should remember him.

Statement 2: It is very difficult for families when they lose their loved ones in wars.

Statement 3: He was one soldier among many and we should not forget all the others.

Statement 4: He was a very young man but to the government he was just a disposable resource.

  b Explain which of these statements you think best sums up the ideas in the poem and why. Support your comments by referring in detail to the poem.

6 Some of the ideas in this poem are very similar to those in poems written in the First World War.
  a Identify the similarities of ideas in this poem to those written in the First World War.
  b Make a list of any references you can find to show that this poem was written in modern times.

Now read Dennis Brutus' poem 'For a Dead African' and answer the questions that follow.

'For a Dead African', by Dennis Brutus, is also remembering people who died fighting for freedom and for their country, but this time it is a different kind of war – a war between a country's government and its people. This poem is about heroes who are not remembered but who are just as important as those who are.

For a Dead African

We have no heroes and no wars
only victims of a sickly state
succumbing to the **variegated** sores
that flower under lashing rains of hate.

5 We have no battles and no fights
for history to record with **trite** remark
only captives killed on eyeless nights
and accidental dyings in the dark.

Yet when the roll of those who died
10 to free our land is called, without surprise
these nameless unnamed ones will stand beside
the warriors who secured the final prize.

Explanations

succumbing **becoming victims**
variegated **multicoloured**
trite **silly and pointless**

7   The title of this poem is 'For a Dead African'. Who do you think this poem was written about and for?

8   Africa is described as:

> a sickly state
> succumbing to the variegated sores
> that flower under lashing rains of hate.

What impression do you get of Africa from the choice of language in this quotation? Refer to specific words and phrases in the quotation and comment on them.

9   How does the poet suggest that there is nothing heroic about the deaths he describes in the second verse?

10   What point do you think the poet is trying to make in the last two lines of the poem?

11   What do you notice about the organisation of the whole poem? Comment on the use of repetition, rhyme and rhythm and their effect in the poem.

12   Re-read 'We Shall Remember Them' (page 96) and 'For a Dead African' (page 98). These poems are about remembering people who have been involved in fighting for their country (in one way or another), but they are very different.

Explain their similarities and differences. You should comment on:
● the context for each poem
● what each poem is saying about remembering people who have died fighting for a cause
● the way each poem is written
● which poem you find more interesting and moving, and why.

You could use a table like the one below to help organise your points.

Feature	'We Shall Remember Them'	'For a Dead African'
The context		
What the poem says about remembering		
The way the poem is written		

6 War speeches

You are learning:
- about the persuasive techniques used in speech-writing.

Wars have inspired some famous speeches. Speeches – including war speeches – can have many purposes. Here are some of those purposes with examples.

Purpose	Example
To inform	A teacher giving a talk in assembly about his trip to the Himalayas during the school holiday.
To explain	A teacher explaining to the class how a piece of science apparatus works.
To entertain	A stand-up comedian telling an amusing story.
To persuade	A charity worker trying to talk someone into making a regular donation.

Activity 1

1 Read extracts A–D, which are all bits of speeches. Each speech has a different main purpose – either to inform, explain, entertain or persuade.

A
Well, you'll never believe it but the third new soldier who arrived in our dug-out was carrying a gold-plated cigarette lighter. 'What do you want that for?' the sergeant asked him. 'It's my lucky charm,' the new soldier replied.

B
Some say we should do a deal with Hitler. I say you can't deal with a cheat. Some say we should let him have Europe. I say we are part of Europe. Some say we cannot beat him. I say we must.

C
I am speaking to you from the Cabinet Room at 10 Downing Street. This morning the British Ambassador in Berlin handed the German government a final note stating that, unless we heard from them by 11 o'clock that they were prepared at once to withdraw their troops from Poland, a state of war would exist between us. I have to tell you now that no such undertaking has been received, and that consequently this country is at war with Germany.

D
War is when two or more opposing groups fight each other over a long period of time. These groups are usually different countries, but that is not always the case. In many parts of the world civil wars are taking place between different tribes or factions in the same country.

2 Write down the letter of each speech (A, B, C or D) and say what the main purpose of that speech is. Briefly explain how you decided on that purpose.

Activity 2

Speeches that are designed to persuade and inspire people tend to use **rhetorical devices**. These are particular methods of persuasion.

1   Look at this list of commonly used rhetorical devices.

- Inclusive pronouns: *we, us, our.*
- Repetition.
- Groups of three: *we want it; we need it; we are going to have it.*
- Rhetorical questions. These are questions that don't need answering: *Are we going to put up with this any longer?*
- Anticipating objections: *I know there are those who will argue that …*
- Giving examples.
- Flow: long sentences that build towards a climax.
- Short sentences for contrast and emphasis.
- Informal language to sound 'down-to-earth'.
- Statistics and 'facts'.
- Vivid images: metaphors and similes.
- Emotive language: words chosen to stir up the listeners' emotions.
- Exaggeration.
- Humour.
- Anecdotes – stories from the speaker's own life.
- Playing on the listener's sense of guilt.
- Claiming special knowledge or authority: *most scientists would agree that …*
- 'Catchy' phrases.

2   Read this speech by Winston Churchill, who became famous for his persuasive, morale-building speeches during the Second World War. As you read the speech notice how he uses rhetorical devices.

Explanations

subjugated defeated
New World United States of America

We shall fight on the beaches…

We shall go on to the end; we shall fight in France; we shall fight on the seas and oceans; we shall fight with growing confidence and growing strength in the air; we shall defend our Island, whatever the cost may be; we shall fight on the beaches; we shall fight on the landing grounds; we shall fight in the fields and in the streets; we shall fight in the hills; we shall never surrender, and even if, which I do not for a moment believe, this Island or a large part of it were **subjugated** and starving, then our Empire beyond the seas, armed and guarded by the British Fleet, would carry on the struggle, until, in God's good time, the **New World**, with all its power and might, steps forth to the rescue and the liberation of the old.

3 Copy the table below and use it to record examples of rhetorical devices used by Churchill. An example has been done for you.

Rhetorical device	Example	Effect
Use of inclusive pronoun	We, we, we	It makes the listener feel that we are 'all in this together' and that will make them feel that the fight will be worthwhile.
Repetition		

Activity 3

The speech that follows comes from William Shakespeare's play *Henry V*. At this point in the play, Henry, who was King of England from 1413 to 1422, is about to lead his troops into battle at Agincourt, France. In order to inspire them he makes this speech telling them that, in the future, they will be proud to have fought in this glorious battle. Although the speech is fictional (we don't know what Henry actually said), it clearly uses rhetorical devices to inspire its listeners. The Battle of Agincourt took place on St Crispin's Day – 25 October 1415.

1 Read King Henry's speech from Shakespeare's play, *Henry V*.

HENRY   This story shall the good man teach his son;
And Crispin Crispian shall ne'er go by
From this day to the ending of the world
But we in it shall be remembered,
We few, we happy few, we band of brothers. 5
For he today that sheds his blood with me
Shall be my brother; be he ne'er so **vile**,
This day shall **gentle his condition**.
And gentlemen in England now a-bed
Shall think themselves accursed they were not here, 10
And hold their manhoods cheap whiles any speaks
That fought with us upon Saint Crispin's day.

Explanations

vile humbly born
gentle his condition
raise him to the rank
of gentleman

Henry V, Act 4 scene 3, William Shakespeare

2 Look at the list of emotions on the right.
  a Explain how Henry's speech appeals to **at least two** of these feelings.
  b What other rhetorical devices does Henry use to persuade his listeners? List some examples and their effects.

pride
fear
shame
comradeship

3   Compare the emotional appeal of Henry's speech with the emotional appeal of recruitment posters A and B on page 94. What similarities do you notice in the way the posters and Henry's speech appeal to their audiences?

Knowledge about language Modal verbs

The common modal verbs are:

could   can   might   may   should   would   ought to   must   will

Modal verbs join with main verbs to give them a sense of doubt or possibility. Here are some examples.

I could [*modal verb*] come [*main verb*] with you
Can [*modal verb*] you play [*main verb*]?
They might [*modal*] like [*main verb*] that film.

1   Which three modal verbs appear in Churchill's speech on page 101?

Be careful: *can*, *might*, *may* and *will* are sometimes used as nouns rather than modal verbs.

2   Modal verbs are particularly useful for exploring ideas and considering alternatives. Look at the two student responses opposite:

Saying America has 'power and might' gives listeners hope.

The modal verbs *could* and *might* have helped the second student to explore alternative meanings and to keep an open mind.

Referring to America's 'power and might' *could* just be a way of reassuring the public, but those words *might* also suggest that Britain is powerless because it has to rely on America's strength in order to survive.

Self-evaluation

Look back over the *Henry V* and 'We shall fight on the beaches' speeches and what you have written about them. Use the criteria below to help you decide how well you have been doing.

Beginner	Competent	Expert
I can identify ways in which writers use language and give some explanation of how their words affect the reader	I can explain in detail (and with appropriate terminology) how language is used	I am beginning to develop a precise, perceptive analysis of how writers choose their language to affect their readers
I can clearly identify how writers persuade their readers	I can explain how the writers' language choices contribute to the overall effect on the reader	I can analyse and evaluate writers' purposes and viewpoints
I can clearly identify writers' purposes and give some explanation of how these are pursued by the writers	I can clearly identify the effect on the reader, and explain to how that effect has been created, commenting on single words or sentences	I can appreciate how particular techniques and devices achieve the effects they do

7 Writing your own speech

You are learning:
- to control the response of your listeners by using rhetorical devices for deliberate effect.

It is essential that you choose your words carefully when you are trying to persuade someone. There are many words in the English language that 'mean' the same thing but have quite different effects or 'shades of meaning'. These are known as a word's **connotations**.

Activity 1

The table below shows how different versions of the same word can have different connotations.

Hot and dramatic		Cool and neutral
mob	gang	crowd
evil		naughty
	hungry	peckish
adore		

Copy the table and fill in the gaps with suitable words.

Activity 2

When writing a speech you need to vary your words, choosing them carefully for effect. You might, for example, mix impressive-sounding words with blunt and direct ones.

1 Read the extract opposite. It is part of a speech made by Winston Churchill on 13 May 1940. Churchill's purpose was to raise the morale of the British people and to make them believe they could win the war.

Let us go forward together with our united strength.

We have before us an ordeal of the most grievous kind. We have before us many, many long months of struggle and of suffering. You ask, what is our policy?

I can say: it is to wage war, by sea, land and air, with all our might and with all the strength that God can give us; to wage war against a monstrous tyranny, never surpassed in the dark, lamentable catalogue of human crime. That is our policy. You ask, what is our aim?

I can answer in one word: it is victory, victory at all costs, victory in spite of all terror, victory, however long and hard the road may be; for without victory, there is no survival.

2 The speech uses a number of impressive-sounding words. Use a table like the one below to explore Churchill's word choices. You will find a dictionary and thesaurus useful for this task. Include the words on the right.

ordeal
struggle
suffering
policy
monstrous
grievous
tyranny
surpassed
lamentable

Churchill's word	Meaning	Alternative words
'ordeal'	A difficult and perhaps painful experience	*hardship, task, trial*

Activity 3

1 Now imagine that you are in one of the following situations.

Situation 1
You are captain of the school football team. It is half time in an important match and you are being beaten by your arch rivals. Your team-mates are down-hearted and lacking self-belief.

Situation 2
You are the leading actor in a school play. It is the interval in the play. The first half was dreadful, with actors forgetting their lines, props falling over and the audience laughing for the wrong reasons.

2 Choose one situation, or a similar situation of your own, and write a speech to encourage people to perform better in the second half.

Remember to:
- use a range of rhetorical devices (see the list of devices on page 101)
- choose your words carefully
- vary your language – mix impressive-sounding words with blunt and direct ones
- vary your sentence structure for impact.

Knowledge about language Semi-colons

Semi-colons can be used instead of a full-stop to signal that the two sentences belong together; one explains the other. Look at these versions of the same sentence:

Version A The soldiers arrived. The villagers hid.
Version B The soldiers arrived; the villagers hid.

In version A there may be no connection between the two actions, but version B hints that the villagers hid *because* the soldiers arrived; the semi-colon signals that one statement is caused by the other.

Rewrite the following sentences so that each one is two statements separated by a semi-colon.

a Because it was raining, he took an umbrella.
b The plane was late because of the bad weather.
c As no one was home she left a note.

Talking and Listening Activity
Listening and responding

'A stand for peace, not a rush for war'

Your task

Listen to the speech made by Alex Salmond in the House of Commons in March, 2004. The United Nations had been looking for weapons of mass destruction in Iraq. When Salmond made the speech, America had led the invasion of Iraq despite there being no weapons found. In the speech, Salmond explains why he was opposed to this invasion and Britain's part in it. (At the time, Alex Salmond was still an MP at Westminster and not the First Minister of the Scottish Parliament which he became in May 2007.)

Listen carefully for:
- rhetorical devices
- how Salmond develops and tries to win his argument.

At the end of each paragraph there is a question to help you summarise Salmond's argument in your own mind. You can make notes in any way you like during the speech, but remember that you won't be able to write down every word.

Alex Salmond on war with Iraq.

Fundamentally, the debate is not about Iraq, **Saddam Hussein**, weapons of mass destruction or even oil, though oil is certainly a factor. The debate is about a new world order, with an unrivalled superpower adopting a doctrine of **pre-emptive strike**. Eighteen months ago the United States had an atrocity committed against it and it is still in a trauma. The point was made a few minutes ago, and it is undoubtedly correct: on 12 September 2001, the day after the attack on the twin towers, the United States was at its most powerful. In addition to its unrivalled military might, it carried total moral authority throughout the world. A hundred or more nations signed messages of sympathy, support or solidarity with the extremity that the United States had suffered.

Explanations

> **Saddam Hussein** the President of Iraq at the time
> **pre-emptive** attacking first before the other side does
> **coalition** group of countries working in partnership
> **dissipated** split up

What does Salmond feel the real issues of the war are?

Now, 18 months later, that enormous world **coalition** has been **dissipated**. I accept that there are more countries – or at least countries' governments – who are signed up, but the coalition of the willing for the campaign against Iraq is very narrowly based. Anyone who wants confirmation of that should just count the troops: 300,000 United States and British troops, and I understand that 1,000 Australians have been asked for, and 100 Poles have been offered. That is a very narrowly based coalition indeed.

How widespread does Salmond feel the support for the war really is?

In his undoubtedly powerful speech today, the **prime minister** argued that the weapons inspection process had never worked. He came close to saying that it had all been a waste of time. I remember a speech on 2 October at the Labour conference in which another powerful speaker went into enormous detail to show how successful the weapons inspection process had been in the 1990s and how it had led to the destruction of chemical weapons, the chemicals used to make weapons, the armed warheads and the biological weapons facility. He concluded that 'the inspections were working even when he' – Saddam Hussein – 'was trying to thwart them.'

I watched that speech on television. The speaker was **President Bill Clinton**. The television was doing cutaways to Ministers, including the prime minister. They were all nodding vigorously. The prime minister now seems to be denying what he accepted only last October.

Does Salmond feel that the Prime Minister is being honest?

We are told that the majority of the **security council** would have voted for the **second resolution**, if it had not been for the nasty French coming in at the last minute and scuppering the whole process. Let us get real. Have we listened to what other countries were saying? The Chileans proposed an extension of three weeks, but they were told by the United States that that was not on. In the **debate in the general assembly**, country after country expressed their anxieties about not letting the weapons inspectors have a chance to do their work. They were told that the nasty French were being extremely unreasonable. The majority of smaller countries in the security council and the general assembly countries did not want to rush to war because they saw that there remained an alternative to taking military action at this stage of the inspection process.

Explanations

prime minister Tony Blair
President Bill Clinton the previous president of America
security council countries in the United Nations
second resolution war
debate in the general assembly United Nations debate

Does Salmond feel that there was a rush into the war?

Will the approach that is being taken work? The argument is that a dictator will be taught a lesson and that that will help us in dealing with other dictators. I do not think that the policy of teaching one dictator a lesson and then moving on to other dictators can work. Most of us know that it will be a breeding ground for a future generation of terrorists. That is not the case because people like Saddam Hussein. The images that will be shown throughout the Muslim world will not feature him, although, without any question, he will be more attractive as a martyr when he is dead than he has ever been while alive. The images that will be shown are those of the innocents who will undoubtedly die in a conflict that will be a breeding ground for terrorism.

Does Salmond feel that getting rid of Saddam Hussein would help?

We are told that the prime minister – this is the essence of his case – will try to restrain some elements in the United States Administration and make them take a **multilateral approach**, but that, if that does not happen, when push comes to shove he has to go along with their policy. I say that there is a broader United States of America than the United States government. I believe that many sections of opinion in America would welcome a vote from this parliament today that says 'Not in our name', because the real America wants to see a stand for peace, not a rush for war.

Explanations

multilateral approach acting together with other countries

Does Salmond believe everyone in the USA wants the war?

Now write answers to the following questions:

1 Why does Alex Salmond believe that the war has been started?

2 What does Salmond think of Britain's part in the war?

3 Does he think that many other countries supported the war? Provide some evidence for your answer.

4 What is the main purpose of the speech?

5 In paragraph 1, how does he make us feel sympathy for what happened to America during the Twin Towers attack?

6 'We are told that the majority of the security council...' (Paragraph 4)
   Explain how and why Salmond mixes formal and informal words in this paragraph.

7 'Will the approach that is being taken work?...' (Paragraph 5).
   What does Salmond mean by describing Saddam Hussein as a 'martyr'?

8 Read Paragraph 6 (that begins 'We are told that the prime minister...'). Write down the phrase that suggests that not everyone in the United States of America wants war.

9 Identify five different ways in which Salmond attempts to persuade his listeners. For each of these, write at least one example as evidence. Use a table like the one below to explore the different ways Salmond attempts to persuade his listeners and the effects they have.

Way of persuading (rhetorical device)	Example(s)	Effects
1		
2		
3		
4		
5		

10 Explain two ways in which Salmond makes his argument easy to follow for the listeners.

11 What is your opinion of Salmond's arguments? Write a letter to Alex Salmond to explain what you agree and/or disagree with about his speech. Make and develop at least three clear points in your letter.

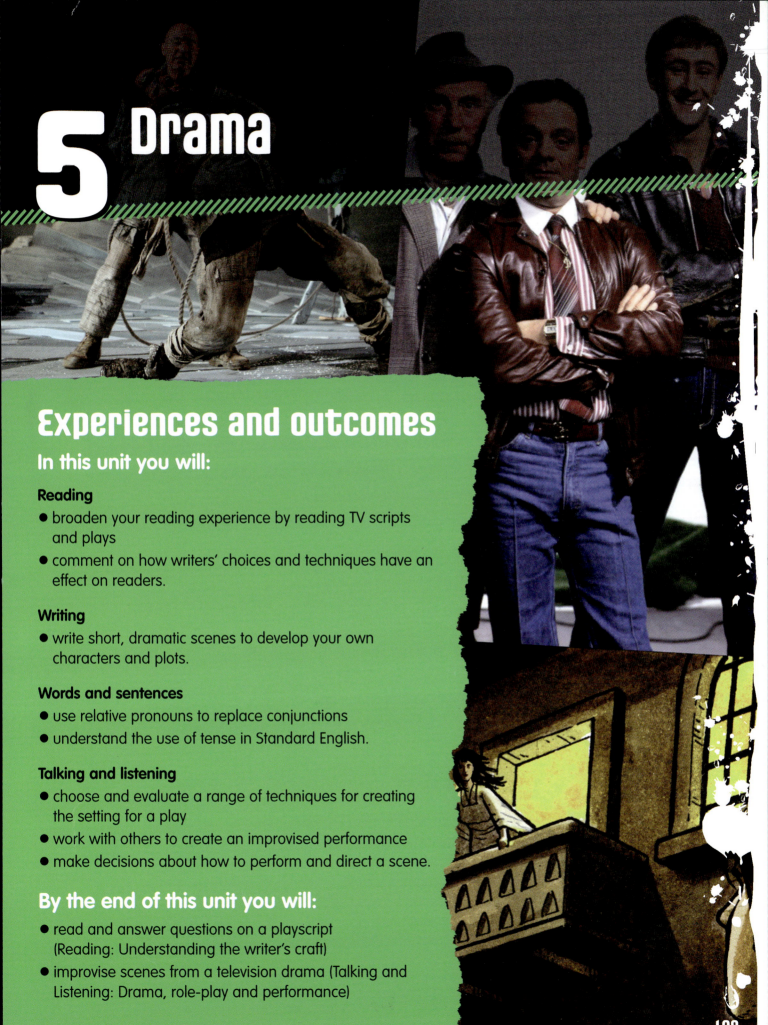

5 Drama

Experiences and outcomes

In this unit you will:

Reading
- broaden your reading experience by reading TV scripts and plays
- comment on how writers' choices and techniques have an effect on readers.

Writing
- write short, dramatic scenes to develop your own characters and plots.

Words and sentences
- use relative pronouns to replace conjunctions
- understand the use of tense in Standard English.

Talking and listening
- choose and evaluate a range of techniques for creating the setting for a play
- work with others to create an improvised performance
- make decisions about how to perform and direct a scene.

By the end of this unit you will:
- read and answer questions on a playscript (Reading: Understanding the writer's craft)
- improvise scenes from a television drama (Talking and Listening: Drama, role-play and performance)

1 Playscripts

You are learning:
- to identify how playscripts are different from other genres of writing.

A playscript is like an instruction book written for directors and actors. It helps them create a performance. A playscript should provide the following information:
- which characters appear in the play
- which characters say which lines
- stage directions describing some of the characters' movements and how they could deliver their lines.

Activity 1

Look at the playscript and short story extract.

1   How are they visually different?

2   What information do you notice at the start of the playscript? How does this immediately tell you what type of text this is?

> *MARY transforms herself into her MAMMY with clothing e.g. a hat from her message bag and squares up to MISS MACKAY.*
>
> **MAMMY:** She's eight year auld and she cannae read nor write yet?
>
> **MISS MACKAY:** She lacks concentration.
>
> **MAMMY:** She's lazy d'ye mean?
>
> **MISS MACKAY:** No, I don't think she's lazy; there is a genuine difficulty here. *(Reading from a sheet of paper)*
>
> Chronological age 8.7… Reading age 6.2 … Spelling age … 5.7 … Verbal reasoning …
>
> **MAMMY:** Well whit are yous gonnae dae aboot it?
>
> **MISS MACKAY:** We could get her some extra help from Learning Support.
>
> *MAMMY changes back into MARY.*
>
> **MARY:** They were nice tae me at furst, but ah couldne dae the hings she wis geein me and she began tae get a bit scunnered. Ah could never tell them aboot the letters diddlin aboot, and naebdy ever asked me whit it wis like. They just gied me tests. Naebdy ever asked me whit wis gaun oan in ma heid. So ah never tellt them. And efter a while the extra lessons stopped.

Extract from the playscript 'Hieroglyphics' by Anne Donovan

Ma mammy thoat ah wis daft, naw, no daft exactly, no the way wee Helen fae doon the street wis. Ah mean she didnae even go tae the same school as us an she couldnae talk right an she looked at ye funny and aw the weans tried tae avoid playin wi her in the street. Ma mammy knew ah could go the messages an dae stuff roond the hoose and talk tae folk, ah wis jist daft at school subjects, the wans that that involved readin or writin oanyway. Fur a while efter she went up tae see the teacher ah got some extra lessons aff the Remmy wummin but ah hated it. She wis nice tae me at furst but then when ah couldnae dae the hings she wis geein me she began tae get a bit scunnered. A hink she thoat A wis lazy, and ah could never tell them aboot the letters diddlin aboot, and oanyway, naebdy ever asked me whit it wis like. They gave me aw these tests an heard ma readin and tellt ma ma ah hud a readin age of 6.4 an a spellin age of 5.7 and Goad knows whit else, but naebdy ever asked me whit wis gaun oan in ma heid. So ah never tellt them.

Activity 2

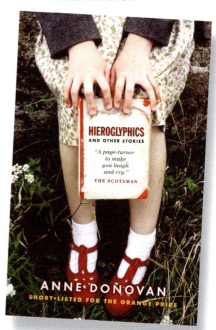

An extract frm the short story 'Hieroglyphics' by Anne Donovan

Novels and short stories are designed to be read by one person at a time. Playscripts are designed to be performed by a group of people, who each take a role.

1   Read the playscript and the paragraph from the short story 'Hieroglyphics'. Answer the questions below to explore how the same story is told in different ways.
    a   Whose viewpoint is the short story told from? Why does this have to change in the play?
    b   Why do you think the playwright chose to make the same character play Mary and her mother?
    c   What additional information does the story give us about Mary's mother that the play does not provide?
    d   Why does 'the Remmy wummin' in the story become 'Learning Support' in the play?

2   Compare how the play is set out compared with the short story. Mention how the characters are introduced; how you know where and when the action is taking place; and how it is set out on the page.

Self-evaluation

Read your answer to question 2 and use the table below to decide your level of understanding. What could you have included in your explanation to improve your level?

Beginner	Competent	Expert
I understand that a novel and a playscript are different and I can name two differences between the two types of writing	I understand how a playscript and novel are different and can give examples of the differences between them	I understand how a playscript and novel are different and can comment on why they are different

2 Settings and openings

You are learning:
- to explore how stage settings can be created and openings can grab an audience's attention.

A story can take its audience anywhere: to every corner of the world, to the edge of the universe. A theatre stage is a small space in which to tell these stories.

Patrick Stewart as Prospero and John Light as Caliban in *The Tempest*

Activity 1

The setting for a play is suggested by the stage set with painted scenery and props, lighting and sound effects. Using only one prop, plus lighting and sound effects, write a short description of how you could suggest the following settings to an audience:

	One prop	Lighting	Sound effects
A school playground			
A city at night			
A deserted graveyard at night			
A busy beach in summer time			

Activity 2

The stage is set, the curtain goes up and you must grab your audience's attention with your opening scene. Shakespeare is perhaps the most influenial of all playwrights, and he opens many of his plays with very dramatic first scenes.

Romeo and Juliet

Act 1 Scene 1: a huge and bloody sword fight between two feuding families

Macbeth

Act 1 Scene 1: three strange old women around a witches' cauldron, chanting threateningly

Hamlet

Act 1 Scene 1: the ghost of the recently deceased King is seen walking the battlements of his castle

1   Select one of these opening scenes. Describe which props, lighting and sound effects you could use, explaining your choices.

2   Read this summary of *The Hound of the Baskervilles* by Sir Arthur Conan Doyle. Which of the characters or incidents would you focus on in an opening scene to grab your audience's attention?

Sir Charles Baskerville is dead. He seems to have fallen victim to the curse of the Baskervilles: a ghostly, ferocious black hound roams the lonely moors of Devon around the old family home, killing any family member who comes to live there. Sir Charles' nephew, Henry, is due to move into the house. A family friend, Dr Mortimer, asks the great detective Sherlock Holmes to solve the mystery and save Henry's life.

3   Design the set for your opening scene from *The Hound of the Baskervilles*. How would you use scenery, props, lighting and sound effects to create the scene and atmosphere for the characters and events you have chosen?

In the opening scene...	Scenery	Props	Lighting	Sound effects

3 Character

You are learning:
- to explore how a playwright presents and develops characters.

Romeo and Juliet is one of Shakespeare's best known plays. Both Romeo and Juliet are young and in love with each other. However, their families – the Capulets and the Montagues – are sworn enemies. Readers interpret the characters in different ways, but many see Romeo as dreamy and romantic, while Juliet is more realistic and practical.

Activity 1

1 Read the following extract from Act 2 Scene 2 – the famous balcony scene. Romeo (a Montague) and Juliet (a Capulet) have met for the first time earlier that night at the Capulet ball. Desperate to see Juliet again, Romeo risks his life by climbing into the Capulet grounds.

JULIET
My ears have not yet drunk a hundred words
Of that tongue's utterance, yet I know the sound:
Art thou not Romeo and a Montague?

ROMEO
Neither, fair saint, if either thee dislike.

JULIET
How camest thou hither, tell me, and wherefore?
The orchard walls are high and hard to climb,
And the place death, considering who thou art,
If any of my kinsmen find thee here.

ROMEO
With love's light wings did I o'er-perch these walls;
For stony limits cannot hold love out,
And what love can do that dares love attempt;
Therefore thy kinsmen are no **let** to me.

JULIET
If they do see thee, they will murder thee.

ROMEO
Alack, there lies more peril in thine eye
Than twenty of their swords: look thou but sweet,
And I am proof against their enmity.

JULIET
I would not for the world they saw thee here.

Explanation

let hindrance

2 Copy and complete the table about Juliet below. Find quotations from the extract above to support the statements. One has been done for you.

Quotation	Statement about Juliet's character
	Juliet immediately knows that Romeo is talking to her, even though she cannot see him.
'I would not for the world they saw thee here'	Juliet cares for Romeo: she worries that he is in terrible danger.
	Juliet wants to know how Romeo has managed to get into the grounds of her family home.

3 Now complete the table below about Romeo. This time you need
to explain what you think the quotations might show about
Romeo's character. One example has been done for you.

Quotation	Statement about Romeo's character
'For stony limits cannot hold love out'	Romeo is in love, and feels that nothing can keep him from his love, Juliet.
'fair saint'	
'With love's light wings did I o'er perch these walls'	
'there lies more peril in thine eye Than twenty of their swords'	

Activity 2

Write a paragraph comparing and contrasting the characters
of Romeo and Juliet as they are presented in this scene.
Use quotations to support your points, remembering to use speech
marks.

Activity 3

Write a short scene, developing two distinctly different characters.
Here are some possibilities:

A hardworking student with a tendency to panic for no reason is discussing a test with a relaxed and laid back friend.

A well-behaved student and a more rebellious student are talking about breaking a school rule – such as going somewhere that is officially out of bounds.

Knowledge about language Past tense to present tense

The following sentences have been written in either the past or present tense.
a   He walked past slowly.
b   The contestants push past, trying to be seen.
c   She stands with an air of dignity around her.
d   The group walks over to where their friends are.
e   The class did not notice the knock at the door.

1   Identify which sentences are written in the past tense and which ones
    in the present tense.

2   Change the tense:
    • put the sentences in the present tense into the past tense
    • put the sentences in the past tense into the present tense.

4 Conflict

You are learning:
- how a playwright creates and develops conflict between characters.

Playwrights can create drama and tension in different ways. In *Romeo and Juliet,* Shakespeare uses the deadly feud between the Montagues and Capulets to create a great deal of conflict between the characters in the play.

Activity 1

1   Read the extract opposite from Act Three Scene One. Juliet's cousin, Tybalt, is furious that Romeo and other Montagues attended the Capulet ball in disguise. He challenges Romeo to a swordfight. Mercutio – Romeo's friend – comes to his defence.

Explanations

villain person of low birth
Alla stoccata a term used in fencing meaning a sudden thrust

TYBALT	Romeo, the hate I bear thee can afford No better term than this – thou art a **villain**.
ROMEO	Tybalt, the reason that I have to love thee Doth much excuse the appertaining rage To such a greeting: villain am I none; Therefore farewell; I see thou know'st me not.
TYBALT	Boy, this shall not excuse the injuries That thou hast done me; therefore turn and draw.
ROMEO	I do protest, I never injured thee, But love thee better than thou canst devise, Till thou shalt know the reason of my love: And so, good Capulet, which name I tender As dearly as my own, be satisfied.
MERCUTIO	O calm, dishonourable, vile submission! **Alla stoccata** carries it away. [Draws his sword] Tybalt, you rat-catcher, will you walk?

2 What expressions does Tybalt use in this extract to try to get Romeo to respond angrily?

3 How does Romeo reply to Tybalt's insults?

4 How does Mercutio show, through his words and actions, that he thinks Romeo is wrong to reply in this way?

Activity 2

Another way to create drama in a scene and to keep the audience interested is through the use of dramatic irony. This is when the audience knows something that one or more characters on the stage do not.

1 Read this description of events in the play up to Act Three Scene One.

2 How does this information change your response to Romeo and his refusal to fight Tybalt?

3 Explain why Tybalt's insults and Romeo's replies are examples of dramatic irony.

> Romeo and Juliet meet for the first time at the Capulet ball, which Romeo has attended in secret. They instantly fall in love and wish to be married to each other. Because of the deadly feud between their families, the marriage takes place in secret. The only people who know about the marriage are Romeo, Juliet, the Friar and the Nurse.

Activity 3

Look again at the extract from Act Three Scene One on page 116. How do you think the audience might respond to each of the characters in this scene? Copy and complete the table below. An example has been done for you.

Character	Audience's response (like/dislike, mixed)	Reason for this response
Tybalt	Dislike	Tybalt has started this argument for no good reason.
Romeo		
Mercutio		

Self-evaluation

Use the table below to decide what level you are working at.

Beginner	Competent	Expert
I can explain why I prefer one character to another	I can describe what a character is like, giving evidence from the text to support my opinion	I can discuss how effectively a writer develops character through their words and actions

5 Choices and decisions

You are learning:
● how decisions a character makes shape a drama.

In plays, the main characters are often faced with important and difficult decisions that have consequences for the rest of the play. Romeo eventually does fight Tybalt – and kills him. Juliet then has to choose between Romeo and her family.

Activity 1

1 Read the extract opposite in which Juliet is speaking to her trusted old servant, who is referred to as 'Nurse'.

2 Look at Juliet's second speech beginning with 'O serpent heart …'. Who is she talking about?

Explanation

forget it fain like to forget it

NURSE	Tybalt is gone, and Romeo banished; Romeo that kill'd him, he is banished.
JULIET	O God! did Romeo's hand shed Tybalt's blood?
NURSE	It did, it did; alas the day, it did!
JULIET	O serpent heart, hid with a flowering face! Did ever dragon keep so fair a cave? Beautiful tyrant! fiend angelical! Dove-feather'd raven! wolvish-ravening lamb! …
NURSE	Shame come to Romeo!
JULIET	Blister'd be thy tongue For such a wish! he was not born to shame: Upon his brow shame is ashamed to sit; For 'tis a throne where honour may be crown'd Sole monarch of the universal earth. O, what a beast was I to chide at him!
NURSE	Will you speak well of him that kill'd your cousin?
JULIET	Shall I speak ill of him that is my husband? Ah, poor my lord, what tongue shall smooth thy name, When I, thy three-hours wife, have mangled it? But, wherefore, villain, didst thou kill my cousin? That villain cousin would have kill'd my husband: Back, foolish tears, back to your native spring; Your tributary drops belong to woe, Which you, mistaking, offer up to joy. My husband lives, that Tybalt would have slain; And Tybalt's dead, that would have slain my husband: All this is comfort; wherefore weep I then? Some word there was, worser than Tybalt's death, That murder'd me: I would **forget it fain**; But, O, it presses to my memory, Like damned guilty deeds to sinners' minds: 'Tybalt is dead, and Romeo – banished;' That 'banished,' that one word 'banished,' Hath slain ten thousand Tybalts.

3 **a** List the words and expressions that show the strength of Juliet's anger.
   b Choose two of these words and expressions and explain what makes them convey her anger powerfully.

4 How does Shakespeare show that Juliet is confused about her feelings?

Activity 2

In the final speech of this extract, Juliet has made her decision.

1 What choice does she make about who she loves more – Tybalt or Romeo?

2 Which lines show this most clearly? Give reasons for your choice.

3 Do you think Juliet makes the right decision? Give reasons for your answer. (Think about what you already know about Tybalt and Romeo.)

Activity 3

Write a short scene in which one or more characters have to make an important decision. You could use one of the scenarios below or come up with an idea of your own. Before you start writing, think about:
● the possible consequences of the decision
● how the character feels about having to make this decision
● what words and expressions you might use to show the dilemma that the character faces.

> A fourteen year old is offered alcohol at a party by an eighteen year old. He/She wants to impress the eighteen year old but doesn't want to drink.

> A pupil is bullying another pupil. The first pupil's friend has to decide whether to say nothing, join in or stop the bullying.

Knowledge about language Joining sentences using who, which, that, whom

> 'My husband lives, that Tybalt would have slain.
> And Tybalt's dead that would have slain my husband.'

You already know that you can link sentences using a connective. 'Romeo is still alive **although** Tybalt tried to kill him.'
Another way of linking these two sentences would be:
'Romeo, whom Tybalt tried to kill, is still alive.'

Rewrite these sentences, using who or which rather than a connective.
1 Juliet is a Capulet **and** is in love with Romeo, a Montague.
2 Juliet was fond of her cousin **but** chooses to be loyal to her husband.
3 Juliet thinks she will never see Romeo again **and** this makes her miserable.

6 Comedy

You are learning:
- to understand the features of comedy as a genre of drama, using situation comedies as an example.

Sitcom, or situation comedy, is a genre of comedy, often produced and shown in a series of episodes. Each episode features the same characters involved in humorous story lines, in a common setting, such as a family home or workplace. Sitcoms were originally devised for radio but today are found mostly on television.

Situation comedies (sitcoms) are programmes that:
- are meant to make you laugh
- often focus on family life
- are sometimes set in the workplace
- have few sets, which are used over and over again
- tend to be shown during peak viewing times
- are often realistic
- appeal to a family audience
- tend to last for half an hour
- are shown at the same time every week
- are easy to understand
- are entertaining
- sometimes have **canned laughter**.

Activity 1

1 Think of as many sitcoms as you can, both American and British. Do they fit all or most of the statements above?

2 Using the statements above, write a definition of a sitcom.

Activity 2

1 *Only Fools and Horses* is a sitcom written by John Sullivan. Read this extract from one of his scripts.

Explanation

canned laughter the sound of recorded laughter, played during situation comedies to encourage viewers to laugh

Internal day. Sid's café
Trigger has been awarded a medal and is very proud of his achievement.

Trigger   It's Councillor Murray's idea. She's head of Finance and Facilities at the Town Hall and she says local people should be rewarded for services to the community. A proud moment in my family's history.

Boycie   Trigger, you haven't got a family history. You were created by a chemical spillage at a germ warfare plant somewhere off Deptford High Street.

Trigger	Maybe. But I still feel proud.
Rodney	So what exactly is the medal for?
Trigger	For saving the council money. I happened to mention to her one day that I've had the same broom for the last twenty years. She was very impressed and said 'Have a medal. Twenty years. Long time, Dave.'
Rodney	Yeah, I know, it's two decades innit?
Trigger	I wouldn't go that far, but it's a long time.
	Sid arrives with teas and things.
Del	If you've had that broom for twenty years d'you ever actually sweep the roads with it?
Trigger	Well of course! But I look after it well. We have an old saying that's been handed down to generations of road sweepers: 'Look after your broom …'
Rodney	*(Finishes off saying for him)* And your broom will look after you.
Trigger	… No Dave. It's just 'Look after your broom.'
Rodney	Oh that old saying!
Trigger	Yeah. And that's what I've done. Maintained it for twenty years. This old broom's had seventeen new heads and fourteen new handles in its time.
Sid	Well, how the hell can it be the same broom then?
Trigger	There's the picture of it! What more proof d'you need?
Boycie	Did you tell this to Councillor Murray about the seventeen new heads and fourteen new handles?
Trigger	No. I didn't get technical with her. Anyway I'll see you around.
Sid	Bon appetite.

From 'Heroes and Villains'
Christmas Special

2 Why is *Only Fools and Horses* often repeated on television?

3 There are lots of ways to make an audience laugh. Can you identify where the writer has used the following techniques in the extract?

Technique	Definition
Mockery	One character makes fun of another
Irony	Sarcasm, used to imply the opposite of what is actually said
Exaggeration	Making something seem greater or more important than it is
Misunderstanding	The difference between a character's understanding and another character's or the audience's understanding
Stupidity	A character's lack of intelligence

4 Choose one example of a technique you have identified in the extract. Write a sentence or two explaining why you think it is funny.

Self-evaluation

How well have you understood the different ways of creating humour?

Beginner	Competent	Expert
I can identify where the writer has tried to create humour	I can identify some of the techniques that the writer has used to create humour	I can identify and comment on some of the techniques that the writer has used to create humour

Reading Activity
Understanding the writer's craft

Gregory's Girl

Gregory's Girl was originally a film. It is about a boy, Gregory, who wants to do well at football so that he can impress Dorothy, a girl he has fallen for. Dorothy is more interested in football than in Gregory and in the end Gregory finds love elsewhere.

This film has been adapted into a playscript for young people to perform.

Your task

Read the opening of *Gregory's Girl* and complete the questions that follow.

The only permanent set is a full-size football goal.
The play begins at the football match. For the other scenes the setting is minimal, but the posts will be used to support simple backdrops to indicate location.

SCENE 1   The first football match

Our school is playing another school. The opposition is much better organised and more skilful.

(ANDY is in goal. He prances hopefully. PHIL, the team coach, stands to the left of the posts, in some anguish, MADELINE and RICHARD are amongst the group of spectators to the right of the posts. The reactions range from desperate encouragement to hoots of derision.)

PHIL   Tackle, will you! Him! For Godsake, tackle him. He's coming inside you. Move. Back. Defence! He's passed it now. Watch the striker. Gregory. GREGORY, watch the striker. ANDY move out. Get off your line, Andy. Now. Dive.

        (Andy is undecided. A shot rifles past him into the net.)

        Oh no! Give me strength.

ANDY   *(Retrieves the ball)* I had it covered.

PHIL	Will you stop laughing, Gregory?
ANDY	Misjudged the swerve.
PHIL	Don't waste time. Kick it back. Still time …
ANDY	Reckon the ball's gone out of shape.
PHIL	Get it back to the centre. Still time to go for a draw.
ANDY	That striker's got to be nineteen.
SPECTATOR	Come on, Barry. Show 'em some elbow. What about a professional foul, Barry. Make it worth our while.
PHIL	Eh! None of that.

(*Whistle. The game restarts.*)

GREGORY	Mark him. MARK HIM!
RICHARD	So why does he play, when he's so bad?
MADELINE	Habit.
RICHARD	I can't see why he can't kick it.
MADELINE	It's complicated. He used to be football mad. Now that he's growing up, you know … 'adolescence'.
RICHARD	Oh that.
MADELINE	He wants to impress. Make an impression on the girls. Trouble is he can't play football to save his life.
RICHARD	You said it, Maddy, not me.
MADELINE	Well one doesn't want to be cruel. It's a difficult time.
RICHARD	So they say.
MADELINE	But he's not going to get very far with the girls playing like that.
RICHARD	And looking like that.
MADELINE	I think his proper shorts are in the wash.
PHIL	Take him, Dawson. Take him. You've given him too much space. He'll run round you. Back. All of you BACK. Go left, Andy. Go left. He always shoots left. Shut down the angle. Move. Now!
MADELINE	It's not easy …
RICHARD	He should have been tackled at the half-way line.
MADELINE	… having an adolescent brother.
RICHARD	I see what you mean.
MADELINE	I try to help.

RICHARD	I'm sure he appreciates it, Maddy.
MADELINE	Oh yes, he appreciates it. I just wish he'd listen.
PHIL	Form up. Move yourselves. There's still time. Chuck it, don't carry it. Alvin, place it. You can't waste time. Take the game to them. Get one back. Salvage some morsel of pride …
	(*The final whistle blows. The game is over.*)
ANDY	Not as bad as Millsborough Tech, sir.
PHIL	Don't push your luck, lad.
ANDY	Better look on the bright side, wouldn't you say?
PHIL	I would not.
ANDY	(*Beginning to walk off*) Are you coming, sir?
PHIL	No!
ANDY	I'd appreciate a post-mortem on that first one.
PHIL	Just go on in and get changed.
ANDY	No need to be so frosty. We did our best.
PHIL	Go!
	(*Andy trots off, not unduly perturbed by this brush-off. Gregory ambles past Phil. He is laughing. Phil throws the ball at Gregory. He drops it.*)
GREGORY	Terrible game, eh?
PHIL	Very bad. Very, very bad.

GREGORY	You've got to laugh.
PHIL	What have you got to laugh at?
GREGORY	Us.
PHIL	It's really that funny, is it?
GREGORY	We're laughable. We're awful. (*Gregory senses a hurt in Phil. He tries to make amends.*) Football is all about entertainment. We give them a good laugh … It's only a game.
PHIL	It's only eight games. Eight games in a row you've lost.
GREGORY	Can't lose them all. You push us really hard, no mercy, lots of discipline, that's what we need. Get tough.
PHIL	We need goals, son, you're not making any goals. That's your job.
GREGORY	Nobody's perfect. It's a tricky time for me. I'm doing a lot of growing, it slows you down. Five inches this year. (*Gregory crouches down so that he's level with Phil, and their faces are very close together.*) Remember last year I was way down here? (*Gregory is still crouching and staring into Phil's face.*) Are you growing a moustache?
PHIL	I want to make some changes.
GREGORY	Good idea. It'll make you look older though.
PHIL	The team. Changes in the team.
GREGORY	You're the boss.
PHIL	I want to try out some other people.
GREGORY	Switch the team around?
PHIL	Take some people out. I was going to take you out.
GREGORY	You don't want to do that.
PHIL	Yes I do.
GREGORY	You don't.
PHIL	I do.
GREGORY	You don't.
PHIL	I might.
GREGORY	Why me?
PHIL	You said yourself you were going through a tricky time. Take a rest.

GREGORY   No … I'm nearly finished growing. Another couple of inches and that'll be me. I'm going to be fine.

(*Phil is silent.*)

What about Andy? He's hardly started growing yet. He's going to be real trouble.

(*Phil is thinking.*)

I'll tell him.

PHIL   I'll tell him. You're in goal. For a trial period of three weeks. That's what I'm telling Andy and that's what I'm telling you.

GREGORY   Have you got a jersey my size? Andy's a lot smaller.

PHIL   Don't worry about the jersey. Three weeks in goal for you and them I'm going to decide.

GREGORY   You're the boss. Who's getting my position?

PHIL   I want to find some new people.

(*Phil turns abruptly, although somewhat aimlessly, and sprints off.*)

GREGORY   (*Calls after him.*) You won't regret this.

(*Gregory goes off, engaged in some elaborate fantasy game.*)

1 The play starts with a football match.

  a Explain how this could be difficult to show on stage, and how you might be able to achieve it.

  b Why do you think the writer decided to open the play with this scene?

  c Think of two ways in which a director could make the first moments of the play, before anyone speaks, exciting and dramatic for the audience.

2 Make notes on Phil's first speech, below, to show his different feelings and how they build up excitement in this opening part of the scene.

> PHIL   Tackle, will you! Him! For Godsake, tackle him. He's coming inside you. Move. Back. Defence! He's passed it now. Watch the striker. Gregory. GREGORY, watch the striker. ANDY move out. Get off your line, Andy. Now. Dive.
>
> (*Andy is undecided. A shot rifles past him into the net.*)
>
> Oh no! Give me strength.

3 What impression do you get of Gregory from this scene? You should refer to and comment on:
   - what Phil says about Gregory
   - what Madeline and Richard say about him
   - what Gregory himself says.

4 How does Madeline and Richard's choice of language suggest that they are more grown-up than Gregory?

  Support your answer by picking out the words and phrases each of them uses and commenting on them.

5 This play is a comedy.

  What techniques does the writer use in this opening scene that are intended to make the audience laugh? Look at the list of techniques on page 121 to help you.

6 Write the next scene of the play, in which Gregory and Madeline are telling their parents about the football match over dinner. You could use these ideas to help you:
   - Their parents are very keen to hear all about the match
   - Gregory uses exaggeration to make his efforts sound more impressive
   - Madeline is reluctant to talk about the game.

7 Improvising a scene

You are learning:
- to work as a group to improvise a scene.

Improvisation means a piece of non-scripted dramatic work that you have made up yourselves. The following activities will encourage you to think on your feet as well as improving your listening and concentration skills.

Activity 1

Imagine that you are one of the characters from the list below. Write down a list of questions that you can answer in role as the character.

- a spoilt child who is trying to get its own way
- a soldier in the British armed forces who is keen to obey
- a famous actor who is bored with answering questions
- an argumentative politician
- a talkative comedian.

Activity 2

1   Read the following guidelines for improvising. The examples are taken from an improvised scene called 'A major incident in the classroom'.

Do	A good example	Don't	A bad example
Plan your characters' attitudes to the situation: conflicting attitudes create drama	Have one character with one attitude and the other with the opposite attitude, e.g. angry and relaxed	Just think about the events in your improvisation	If everyone is angry, the shouting and fighting will get boring for the audience
Enter or exit with a purpose: an action, emotion or attitude	'Sorry I'm late, Miss, but my budgie died this morning. (*sniff*)'	Wander in and hope for the best	'Er...hello.'
Start halfway through the action	'Miss, Miss, Ryan's stolen my best pencil!'	Start with the characters introducing each other	'Good morning, children, my name is Miss Brown and I am your new teacher.'
Build on your partner's improvisation	'Oh Barry, this is the fifth time I've had to speak to you this lesson...'	Deny or disagree with your partner's improvisation	'No you're not, you're the janitor.'
Give lots of detail for your partner to respond to	'...and you've already had three detentions this week!'	Say things to which there are few possible replies	'Stop it, Ryan!'

2 You are going to carry out your own improvisation. The following are possible ideas that you could use for your improvisation.

- school trips
- growing up and not being very good at a particular activity
- unexpected events on public transport
- a group of friends teasing each other.

a Choose one of these ideas – or come up with one of your own.
b Use the table on page 128 to help you decide on the different characters you will have in your improvisation.

Activity 3

Use this flowchart to develop your character. It will help you think of what to say and how to react to what the other actors say. For every question you answer from the flowchart, ask another question from the question bank – and answer it.

Question bank
Why?
What about?
What for?
How does s/he feel about that?
Who does that?
How?
Will that always be true?

1 Choose an emotion that will sum up your character in one word. Are they happy, angry, sad, bored, worried, frightened…?

2 What is your character's job?

3 What has happened to your character so far today? Write three or four sentences from their diary for today. Try to think of dramatic or interesting events.

Worried.
Why? Because she has lied to her mum.
What about? Where she's going tonight.

Amy

Student.
How does she feel about that? She likes school when she does well but sometimes gets annoyed when she doesn't.

Woke up and had an argument with her mum. Left home late and was late for school. Got told off. **How does she feel about that?** Annoyed.

8 What is your character's name?

Laura.
Why? They live on the same street and have been in the same class since Year 1.
Will that always be true? No. Laura is starting to annoy her.

7 Who is your character's best friend? Describe them.

4 What is your character wearing? Describe their clothes. Now add some more adjectives to develop the description.

School uniform. Scruffy. Muddy.
Why? She can't find her clean uniform because her room is a mess.

5 Describe your character's home.

6 Describe your character's family.

Lives with mum, baby sister and hamster. Mum spends all her time and energy on baby sister.
How does she feel about that? A bit jealous and annoyed sometimes.

A small house, kept neat, clean, tidy.
Who does that? Mum works hard all day and then cleans up, which can make her angry.

Activity 4

1   Now that you have developed your characters, use the table on page 128 to think about:
    - how you will start your improvisation
    - how your improvisation might develop.

2   Perform your improvisation.

3   State two positive things about your performance and one thing that you would like to improve. You will work towards meeting this target during the next activity.

Self-evaluation

Below are the Talking and Listening levels. What level do you think your performance was and why?

Beginner	Competent	Expert
• I talked and listened with some confidence • I chose appropriate words and expressions for our performance • I listened carefully to others and responded to what they said	• I talked and listened confidently • I chose good words and expressions to suit our performance • I am beginning to vary my expression and the words I use • I made a relevant contribution and encouraged others to contribute	• I talked and listened confidently • I chose good words and expressions and gave a consistently good performance • I am good at varying my expression and vocabulary • I made a contribution that built on others' ideas and encouraged everybody to contribute

Knowledge about language Future tense

There are two ways of putting a verb into the future tense: by adding 'will' or 'going to' into the verb phrase. For example:

Past tense	Present tense	Future tense
I worked hard on my homework.	I work hard on my homework.	I will work hard on my homework.
I ate a sandwich.	I am eating a sandwich.	I am going to eat a sandwich.

Using the future tense, write down two Talking and Listening targets that you will achieve and say how you will achieve them.
- I will…
- To achieve this I am going to…

8 Performing and directing a scene

You are learning:
- to make decisions about how you would perform and direct a scene.

A good script is only the first step towards a performance. To engage and entertain an audience, the director and the actors must decide how they will perform and deliver the script.

Activity 1

1 Facial expressions tell an audience a lot about how a character is feeling and what they are thinking. What do these facial expressions suggest to you?

2 Read this short drama extract.

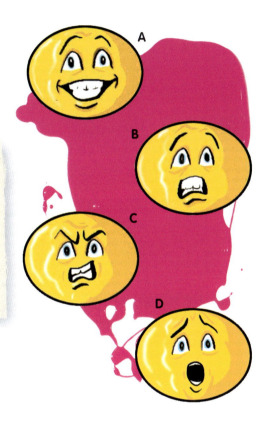

> Alan: I can't believe it.
> Caitlin: What's happened?
> Alan: They said this would never happen and it has.
> Caitlin: What is it? What is it?
> Alan: I told them it would, but they didn't believe me.
> Caitlin: And you were right?
> Alan: I usually am.

3 What do you think has happened? How are these characters feeling?

4 Draw a face for each line of the script, showing the expression you think the actor should use. Try to use as many different emotions as possible.

Activity 2

1 Look at this diagram of an actor. What feelings is it trying to represent?

2 Draw a character diagram for each of the lines in the extract above, showing how the actors should use body language to support their facial expressions.

3 What other advice would you give the actors performing this scene? Think about tone of voice and pace (the speed at which they deliver their lines and any pauses).

131

Activity 3

1 Read this extract from Shakespeare's *Macbeth*. Macbeth and his wife are deciding whether to go through with the murder of King Duncan.

MACBETH	Prithee, peace:
	I dare do all that may become a man;
	Who dares do more is none.
LADY MACBETH	What beast was't, then,
	That made you break this enterprise to me?
	When you durst do it, then you were a man;
	And, to be more than what you were, you would
	Be so much more the man. Nor time nor place
	Did then adhere, and yet you would make both:
	They have made themselves, and that their fitness now
	Does unmake you. I have given suck, and know
	How tender 'tis to love the babe that milks me:
	I would, while it was smiling in my face,
	Have pluck'd my nipple from his boneless gums,
	And dash'd the brains out, had I so sworn as you
	Have done to this.
MACBETH	If we should fail?
LADY MACBETH	We fail!
	But screw your courage to the sticking-place,
	And we'll not fail.

2 Which character wants to murder Duncan and which character has doubts? Give evidence from the passage for your choice.

3 Is Lady Macbeth saying that:
   ● Macbeth would be more manly if he were a murderer
   ● if Macbeth killed the king and became King himself he would be a more important man
   ● both?
   Give reasons for your choice.

4 Work in pairs to try out different ways of saying these lines.
   a Look at Macbeth's first speech. Does Macbeth say it timidly – is he quite nervous of his wife? Does he say it angrily, trying to dominate her? Try saying it both ways.
   b Look at Lady Macbeth's first speech. It contains some very violent imagery. Try reading it quietly as though she is calm and utterly determined. Then try reading it as though she is hysterical and not entirely in control of her anger. Which works better?

c   Lady Macbeth's 'We fail!' in her final speech could be said in many different ways. Try to convey the following ideas just by the tone in which you say, 'We fail.'
- scornful – obviously they won't fail
- frightened – the consequences will be death for both of them
- resigned – if they fail, they fail
- surprised – this simply hasn't occurred to her before

Activity 4

1   Read the extract opposite where King Duncan has been discovered murdered at Macbeth's castle. Macduff and Lennox are nobles who have come to meet the king. Malcolm is Duncan's son.

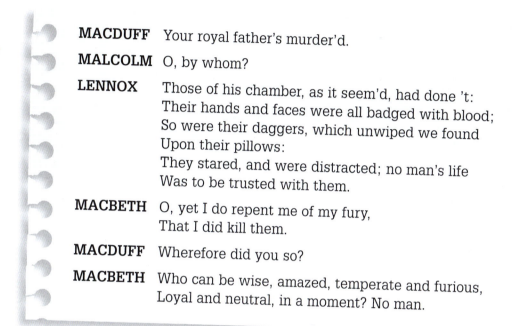

MACDUFF	Your royal father's murder'd.
MALCOLM	O, by whom?
LENNOX	Those of his chamber, as it seem'd, had done 't: Their hands and faces were all badged with blood; So were their daggers, which unwiped we found Upon their pillows: They stared, and were distracted; no man's life Was to be trusted with them.
MACBETH	O, yet I do repent me of my fury, That I did kill them.
MACDUFF	Wherefore did you so?
MACBETH	Who can be wise, amazed, temperate and furious, Loyal and neutral, in a moment? No man.

2   Read this scene again in groups of five. One person should be the director while the other four take a part each. The director should consider the following:

> **1** Where should the actors stand? Is everyone there at the start or would it be better if Macduff and Lennox came in from off-stage? Should the actors stand still as they say their lines or should they walk around? How could you suggest that Macduff has a stronger personality than Lennox? Remember that even when talking to each other, the actors can not have their backs to the audience as no one will hear what they say.

> **2** How should Malcolm say his speech? Should he say the 'O' as a sharp intake of breath? Angrily? Frightened and shocked? What actions should he make to reflect his feelings?

> **3** Should there be pauses? Try asking Macduff to count slowly to ten after Macbeth's first speech while the other actors simply look at him in surprise.

Now change and let someone else be the director. Allow everyone in the group to have a turn and then discuss what you think worked best.

Talking and Listening Activity
Drama, role-play and performance

Where have you been?

Below is the opening of a scene from a television drama. It is about a teenager called David, his sister Jo, and his parents, Diane and Stuart. At the beginning of the scene, David has not returned home in time for dinner.

Diane: Where is he? He knows it's dinner time…

Stuart: He should have phoned but I expect he forgot. Come on, love, let's eat. I'm starving. He'll be back soon…

Diane: I can't relax when I don't know where he is. Why can't he just ring and let us know where he is? His dinner will get cold.

Jo: He'll be back soon, Mum.

Diane: He'd better be…

(The door opens and in comes David wearing a hoodie with the hood up and gloves.)

Diane: Oh, David…

Stuart: There you are, son, we were just wondering where you'd got to. Now come in and have some dinner.

Diane: Where have you been and what have you been up to? Why are you wearing that hood and those gloves?

David: Oh forget it, Mum. What's for dinner?

Your task

Use this scene as the starting point for **two** improvised scenes from a television drama.

In each scene you should:

● develop the characters in different ways
● explore a different idea or create a different mood or atmosphere.

For example, you could focus on relationships between parents and teenagers and the lack of communication between them; you could make it a comedy or a mystery. You don't need to provide an 'ending'; you could end on a cliffhanger or at any point you like. You are only developing part of the whole drama.

You need to remember to:

● develop each character convincingly in two different ways using voice, mannerisms, gestures and movements
● show how the relationships develop differently in each scene
● create a particular mood or atmosphere for the audience in each case.

6 Persuasion

Experiences and outcomes

In this unit you will:

Reading

- explore a range of ideas and viewpoints, purposes and themes in a variety of texts
- identify techniques used to influence opinions and how writers and speakers persuade their audiences.

Writing

- persuade, argue and evaluate using a clear line of thought and relevant supporting evidence
- use and develop vocabulary, selecting words to suit your audience and purpose.

Talking and Listening

- engage with others, making a relevant contribution, encouraging others to contribute and acknowledging they have the right to hold a different opinion
- select and organise ideas and relevant information and communicate effectively to an audience.

By the end of this unit you will:

- write a discursive persuasive essay
  (Writing Activity: Discursive writing)
- make a persuasive presentation in a group.

1 What really happened?

You are learning:
- how to sequence and combine images and dialogue to create and change narratives.

We should not always believe our eyes. Images and dialogue can be manipulated to make people look better – or worse – and sequences of images can be re-ordered to make a story more interesting or dramatic, or even tell a different story.

Activity 1

Television programmes have often been accused of creating or improving storylines, making real events more dramatic by showing them in a different sequence to the order in which they happened.

How Reality TV Fakes It

Queen furious over 'fake' documentary footage

'Killer' whale caught in fishy editing

1 Look at these clips. What do you think might be the viewers' response to this sequence of events?

A **Video**

Audio **Narrator:** It's 10.20am. Gary, Harry and Fran are in the kitchen. Gary's telling a joke.
Gary: What's red and stands in the corner? A naughty strawberry!

B

Harry: That's quite good.
Fran: D'you know any more?

C

It's 2.40pm. Harry and Fran are in the kitchen feeling bored ...

2 What happens if the editor decides to cut all of shot B and the audio from shot C? The sequence of events becomes: Gary tells a joke; Fran and Harry look really bored. How might this change the viewers' response to:
  a The sequence of events
  b i Gary; ii Harry and Fran?

Activity 2

An editor can swap images around to change a story *and* use **Frankenbiting** to make reality television contestants appear to say things they do not mean.

Explanations

soundbite short audio extract, usually dialogue
Frankenstein fictional creator of a monster made from the body parts of different corpses
Frankenbite two separate video/audio extracts edited together to make a reality television contestant appear to have said something more interesting, dramatic or controversial than they actually said

1 Look at these images, showing an incident from a reality
   television show filmed at a school. The effect of these images can
   be transformed if they are edited into a different sequence.
   a What story has been created in this edited sequence: A-B-F?
   b What story has been created in this edited sequence: C-D-H?

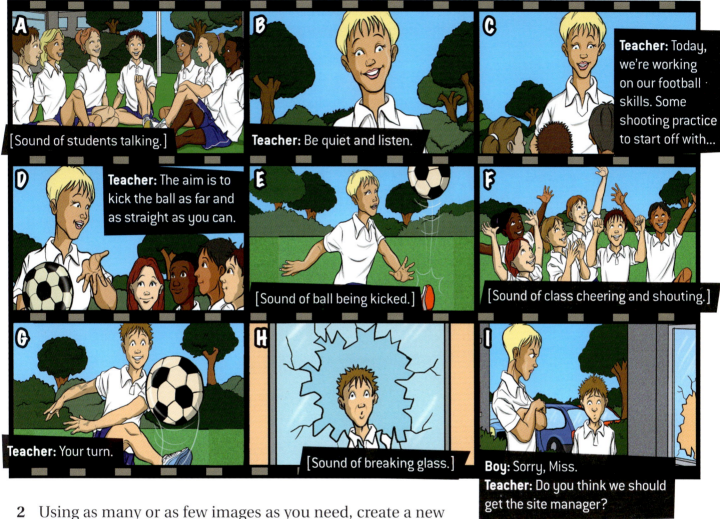

2 Using as many or as few images as you need, create a new
   sequence of images to tell a different story.

3 How could you edit and sequence the audio as well as the
   video to further re-write these events?

Self-evaluation

You have been exploring how programme makers manipulate images and dialogue
to create different meanings. Use the table below to assess how well you are doing.

Beginner	Competent	Expert
I am learning to recognise when a television programme tries to influence me	I am aware of techniques used to influence me and can recognise persuasion	I can identify some of the techniques used to influence and manipulate the audience's response

2 Real lives

You are learning:
- to compare how the media present real people and celebrities.

The media is full of stories about celebrities, and sometimes about 'real' people, too. The stories the media selects, and the way in which they present them, can be very different depending on the status of the characters involved.

Activity 1

1 Read Text A. Who do you think is the intended audience?

Text A

Real life **"MY MAKE-UP TURNED ME INTO A MONSTER"**

A must-have foundation gave Ashley, 13, a brand new look – only it was anything but glam!

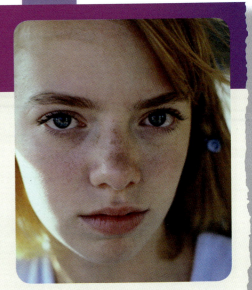

'I used to wear make-up every day. At first, I'd just worn a bit of concealer if I got a zit, but now it had got to the stage where my face felt bare if I wasn't wearing the works, even just to nip out to a local shop.

'One Saturday, I went into town and bought a new dress for a teen disco that night. And of course, I just had to get some new make-up to match it. I splashed out on a glitter eyeliner and eyeshadow, then I spotted a new foundation I'd seen advertised.

'Later the girls met up at my place, so we could all get ready together. The new foundation was fab – it felt quite cool going on and the colour blended so well, my skin looked perfect. Then as I put on my mascara, I noticed something was wrong.

'My right cheek looked a bit swollen. Soon it felt like it was getting worse. My bezzie, Carla*, took one look then went to fetch a cold, wet flannel to hold against it. It didn't do any good. The swelling was starting to spread to the rest of my face.

'Now I really began to panic. I felt short of breath and gasped for air. Carla fetched my mum. I couldn't bear to look at myself in the mirror – my face was so puffed up and red, I looked like a monster.

'My mum took me to A&E. I was given an injection to stop the pain and swelling. Within a couple of hours, I began to look like my normal self again.

'I still love make-up but I never want to go through anything like that again. So I check the labels for the ingredient I react to, or just buy hypoallergenic brands. I take better care of my skin, too – I don't slap on loads of make-up and I make sure I always cleanse properly before I go to bed. I'm much more careful now – I'll do anything, even go make-up free, to avoid risking another flare-up.'

As told to Laura Jones
* Names have been changed to protect identities. Picture posed by a model

2 Why has the writer selected this story to appeal to that audience? Is it because it's dramatic? Funny? Worrying? Gives the reader good advice? Or something else?

3 This story is written in the first person, from Ashley's point of view, and placed within speech marks. Why has the journalist chosen to present the story in this way?

4 Look over your answers to questions 1–3.
   a Which features has the writer used to suggest that this is a 'real' story?
   b In what ways is this story not 'real'?

Activity 2

1 Now read Text B. Who do you think is the intended audience?

Text B

Vicky B. does casual

It's the picture we never thought we'd see – Vicky B. rockin' a pair of baggy jeans, a plain black tee and FLATS!!!

Mrs Beckham, who is famous for her high-octane glamour and designer outfits, dressed down in casual chic for an outing with hubby David and the kids in Disneyland, California.

And while we think this less **contrived** outfit suits Posh surprisingly well, we can't help but wonder if her drastic change of style has anything to do with the promotion of her upcoming range of men's denim for her own label dVb?

Whatever the reason, it must be a breath of fresh air for David to see his wife abandon the straight-off-the-catwalk look for once.

Now, if we could only work on that smile…

2 Why has the writer selected this story to appeal to that audience?

3 What impression of Victoria Beckham is the writer trying to give the reader in this article?

   a Identify two quotations that give a positive impression and two that give a negative impression. Write a sentence or two for each quote, explaining how the writer's choices have created this impression.

   b Why is the writer trying to give a positive **and** a negative impression of Victoria Beckham?

Explanation

contrived carefully thought about and created

Activity 3

1 Look again at Text A and Text B.

   a How would the appeal of the stories change if you swapped their subjects, as below?

      • A wealthy celebrity suffers a terrible allergic reaction to make-up

      • A normal, everyday person goes out in a pair of jeans

   b What does this suggest about how the media select the following?

      i   Real-life stories

      ii Celebrity stories

2 The media sometimes refer to non-celebrities as 'real people' and their stories as 'real' or 'true life'. What does this suggest about celebrities and their stories?

Self-evaluation

1 Write a short article, either about a real life story or a celebrity item. Remember to include the features you have identified in Activities 1 and 2.

2 Annotate your article, showing how you have selected a story to appeal to your audience and used features appropriate for that article.

3 Influencing readers' opinions

You are learning:
- how the writers use language to influence their readers' opinions.

Writers can influence readers' opinions of issues, people and events in different ways. An important way in which they can do this is through the words and phrases they use.

Activity 1

Read the following article from *The Telegraph* and answer the questions that follow.

We shouldn't take pleasure in the plight of Lehman Brothers' employees

By Tracy Corrigan

Women weeping in each others' arms. Grim faces. Frantic phonecalls. Lehman Brothers' 5,000 UK employees learnt on Monday that the distressed US investment bank had filed for bankruptcy.

They have lost their jobs, and may not even receive their pay cheques at the end of the month, let alone any redundancy money.

The images of distress, as staff congregated outside Lehman's shiny office in the heart of Canary Wharf, were poignant.

While the remuneration of investment bankers may be enviable, the lifestyle is often less glamorous than it looks. Like lawyers, investment bankers are at the whim of their corporate clients. They spend much of their lives on planes and in hotels, and when that means lost weekends and constant jet-lag, the pleasure of travelling business class starts to pall. Poor lambs, they are not, but these bankers have made a choice which

people might envy less, if they saw the day-to-day reality. Almost invariably such bankers are men and their wives do not work. The deal is that they make a huge amount of money, but their employer has first call on their time and effort.

From *The Telegraph*, 16th September 2008

1 List all the words and phrases the writer uses in the first three paragraphs to suggest that we should sympathise with employees of Lehman Bank.

2 According to the fourth paragraph, why might most people envy investment bankers rather than feeling sorry for them?

3 What reasons does the writer give for why people should feel sorry for investment bankers rather than envying them?

4 How successful has the writer been in gaining your sympathy for these investment bankers? Justify your answer by referring closely to the article.

Activity 2

Read the article opposite from the *Daily Record*.
For each of the following words, explain what impression it gives of those who work in financial services:

 **a** city slickers    **b** greedy bankers   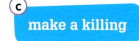 **c** make a killing

Activity 3

Read the following article from *The Independent* and answer the questions that follow.

Short Sell Ban Hits the City Slickers

GREEDY bankers were last night banned from making a killing by 'short selling' shares.

City watchdogs barred the practice of dealers betting on share prices falling.

From *Daily Record*,
19th September 2008

Now we all have to pay for the banks' mistakes

CITY WHIZZKIDS and investment bankers have traditionally benefited from the general inability from the rest of us to understand what they generally get up to.

Once the talk turns to derivatives, short-selling or deleveraging, our eyes glaze over as mine once did when they tried to teach me modern philosophy at Oxford.

This time round, however, the situation is a bit different. Because at the root of the current crisis there is a simple and quite easily grasped fact, namely that banks were lending large sums of money to people who they knew were unlikely to be able to pay it back.

From *The Independent*, Saturday
20th September 2008

1 How does the writer suggest that bankers are different from other people?

2 Why does this make the reader less likely to sympathise with bankers?

3 What does 'whizzkids' mean? By using this term, does the writer make you more or less likely to sympathise with them? Give reasons for your answer.

4 Reread the *Telegraph* article on page 140 again. Has reading the other articles from the *Daily Record* and *The Independent* made you less sympathetic to the bankers losing their jobs? Give reasons for your answer.

4 Reality TV

You are learning:

● about the key features of reality television shows, their purpose and how they appeal to their audience.

At the start of the twenty-first century, a new television genre emerged: reality TV. It has been growing in popularity ever since. Programme makers put ordinary people or celebrities in either competitions or real situations, and film the drama that this creates.

to entertain
to be entertained
to inform
to be informed
to learn
to make money
to become (more) famous
to increase viewing figures
to achieve a challenge

Activity 1

1   Read summaries **A–C** of three different reality television shows. What do you think is the purpose of each programme for each of these groups?

Group a   The viewers.
Group b   The people taking part.
Group c   The programme makers.

You can choose your answers from the suggestions in the box opposite, or add your own.

A

Big Brother

Up to 16 members of the general public live together in a house for about three months. They have no contact with the outside world but are monitored by cameras and microphones at all times. Each day's activities are edited into an hour-long programme. Every week, members of the house nominate a number of housemates for eviction. The public are invited to vote for the nominated housemate they would like to see evicted. The last remaining housemate wins a cash prize.

B

The Apprentice

A powerful, wealthy businessman has a job vacancy in his large corporation. Sixteen men and women, all desperate for the job, compete in teams to succeed in a series of business challenges over several weeks, trying to impress the businessman. Each week, one of the 'apprentices' is fired. The winner is given a job in the large corporation, earning a six-figure salary.

C

The X Factor

Members of the public are auditioned for their singing/ musical ability in venues across the UK. Finalists are chosen and put in categories, e.g. male, female, groups and over 25s. The acts perform a different song each week in front of a live studio and television audience, and the public are invited to vote for their favourite by phone. The two acts with the fewest votes have to sing again and the judges send one of them home. The last remaining act wins a recording contract.

2 Although these programmes have major differences, they also share many common features. Using the information on page 142, copy and complete this table.

	Big Brother	The Apprentice	The X Factor
Who takes part in the show?			
Where is the show set?			
Does the show have rules? What are they?			
Are the viewers involved? How?			
Is there a winner and a prize?			
Is the show 'live' or recorded and edited?			

3 **a** List any other reality television programmes you have seen.
   b Do these shows share the same key features? Select two from your list and identify which of the key features they have.

4 Using your answers to questions **2** and **3**, write a paragraph about the key features of reality television. You could use the following sentence starters:

   All reality shows...
   Some reality shows...
   However, other reality shows...

5 Reality television shows often take real people and place them in artificial or specially created situations. How many of the 'reality' programmes you listed in question 3 are 'real'? Which ones?

6 Write a definition of reality television in two or three sentences.

5 Expressing your point of view

You are learning:
- to plan, structure and write an argument.

As we grow up, we stop believing everything we are told and develop our own opinions. Sometimes we want people to change their opinion and share ours. Expressing an opinion in a written argument needs to be carefully planned and structured, if it is going to influence the opinions of others.

Activity 1

1 Read Esther Rantzen's article below. It expresses her opinions on reality television and compares twenty-first-century TV with the TV of 1968, when she first appeared on our screens.

A curse on cruelty TV!

Back in 1968, when I started out, there were only three channels, no satellites or downloads, no YouTube, no day-time television, no naked boobs, no chat shows.

Since then I've had huge fun working in front of and behind the cameras. My job has taken me behind the scenes of great and glorious events, into hidden places and remote hide-outs, and I've met heroes, villains and the funny, compassionate 'ordinary' people of Britain.

How radically television has changed. Rude interviewers, humiliating formats and unfair editing often reveal a contempt for programme-makers' subjects and for their viewers.

Take *Britain's Got Talent*. Here we see wannabe performers ranging from the brilliant to the absurd. Some are treated with compassion; others are booted off **ignominiously**. While I find myself horribly mesmerised by the most grotesque – and least talented – acts, I wonder why it has to have this edge of cruelty.

Is it just coincidence that bullying is the biggest single problem children bring to **ChildLine**, with 37,000 calls from deeply distressed victims last year alone? Bullying flourishes not just in schools but on our screens, and it's glorified. Once, it would not have been tolerated.

Shows such as *The Weakest Link* have all garnered huge success by creating a modern theatre of cruelty in which contestants are humiliated – and audiences laugh at their expense. Some programmes, such as *The Jerry Springer Show*, seem deliberately to dehumanise them. The schedules are dotted with films about men and women with diseases or disabilities, who are treated like

144

freaks. We are living in the era of 'Mean TV'. These are forums sustained by the modern obsession with celebrity, in which people of little talent make fools of themselves chasing a hopeless dream.

The best programmes – and there are many – prove that the skills that informed programme-making in the 1960s are still there. The brilliance of *The Apprentice* turns each Wednesday night into an event. The glitz and glamour of *Strictly Come Dancing* warms our winter Saturday nights and has been sold around the world, topping the ratings everywhere. Yes, these are reality shows, but they are also beautifully produced. So the good news is that great programmes are still being made.

All the medium needs to do for its survival is to restore respect. Respect for the people who take part in programmes, respect for standards of honesty and, above all, respect for the audiences. Only then will the television industry regain *our* respect, and the pride of place in our lives it had 40 years ago.

Explanations

> **ignominious** shameful, embarrassing
> **ChildLine** free and confidential telephone service for young people in distress

2 Sum up Esther Rantzen's argument in one or two sentences.

3 Look again at paragraphs 1 and 2 of the article.
  a How does Esther Rantzen introduce her argument?
  b What advice would you give another student on 'how to write an introduction' using this as an example?

4 Look again at the final paragraph of the article.
  a How does Esther Rantzen conclude her article?
  b What advice would you give another student on 'how to write a conclusion', using this as an example?

Activity 2

1 a What are the key points made in this article? Where in the paragraph(s) are they placed? You could put your information in a table like the one below.

Paragraph	Key point(s)	Position in paragraph (e.g. start, middle, end)
1		
2		

  b What do you notice about the position of key points? Where are they usually placed in a paragraph or group of paragraphs?
  c What evidence is provided to prove Esther Rantzen's key points? Add an extra column to the table above, entitled 'Evidence to prove it'.

2 Esther Rantzen's opinions are not entirely negative.
  a In which paragraph does she make a positive point about reality television?
  b How can giving opposing opinions strengthen, not weaken, your argument?

145

Activity 3

1   Imagine you have been asked to write an article for a newspaper. Choose one of the topics on the right.

Do you agree or disagree with your chosen statement? Write a sentence or two expressing your opinion.

- Celebrities deserve a private life. The media should leave them alone.
- We should stop worshipping celebrities. They're just normal people.
- Real people are more interesting to watch and read about than celebrities.

2   **a**   Use a spider diagram (like the one below) to develop three different points you could make to express your opinion.

The media think we're interested in every little thing celebrities do. We're not.

Celebrities deserve a private life. The media should leave them alone.

b   Now sequence your points by numbering them on your spider diagram. What would be the best order in which to put them in your argument?

c   Can you think of a point from the opposing argument? Esther Rantzen put her opposing or counter-argument last, just before her conclusion. Number your counter-argument point to show where you will put it in the sequence of your argument.

d   Finally, try to think of examples you can use as evidence for each of your points. Add them to your spider diagram.

Evidence: Last week a magazine published pictures of...

The media think we're interested in every little thing celebrities do. We're not.

3   Look again at your answers to questions 3b and 4b of Activity 1 (page 145). List some ideas of what you could include in:

a   the introduction of your chosen argument

b   the conclusion.

Knowledge about language
Sequencing your paragraphs

When writing an argument, it is important to put your key points into the best sequence. Look at this argument entitled *Reality Television is the Best Television*. How would you order these key points?

A   Why watch actors pretending to be real people when you can watch *real* real people?

B   Reality television is one of the most popular genres on television, watched by millions.

C   Reality television is unpredictable. Even the programme makers don't know what will happen next.

Activity 4

Esther Rantzen uses lots of persuasive language techniques – or rhetorical devices – in her argument to make it more persuasive.

1 a Match the examples to the names of these rhetorical devices.
   b Write a definition explaining the meaning of each one.

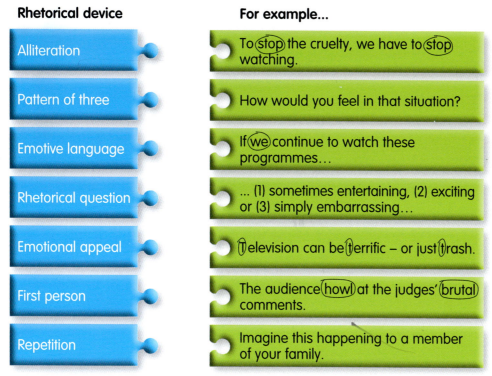

Rhetorical device

Alliteration

Pattern of three

Emotive language

Rhetorical question

Emotional appeal

First person

Repetition

For example...

To (stop) the cruelty, we have to (stop) watching.

How would you feel in that situation?

If (we) continue to watch these programmes…

… (1) sometimes entertaining, (2) exciting or (3) simply embarrassing…

(T)elevision can be (t)errific – or just (t)rash.

The audience (howl) at the judges' (brutal) comments.

Imagine this happening to a member of your family.

2 For each of these rhetorical devices:
   a find one example that Esther Rantzen uses in her article
   b write a sentence or two explaining the effect the writer wants to have on the audience.

Self-evaluation

You have been learning to develop points and use evidence to support your point of view. Use the table below to assess how well you are doing.

	Beginner	Competent	Expert
Selection and organisation	I can select ideas and relevant information and organise these appropriately.	I can select ideas and relevant information and organise these appropriately.	I can independently select ideas and organise these in a logical order.
Language and style	I am beginning to use language to influence and persuade my reader.	I can persuade my reader through my use of language, style and tone.	I can persuade readers through my deliberate choice and use of language, style and tone.
Constructing an argument	I can use relevant supporting detail and evidence to back up my argument.	I can establish a clear line of thought, supported by relevant, detailed evidence.	I can establish a persuasive line of thought, using relevant, detailed evidence to justify my opinion.

6 Taking sides

You are learning:
● how writers create biased texts.

Writers can give a biased view and persuade readers to adopt this view. Writers can do this through choice of language and the details they choose to emphasise to influence their readers' understanding.

Activity 1

1 Read the following article from BusinessGreen.com about the rejection of a wind farm on the Isle of Lewis.

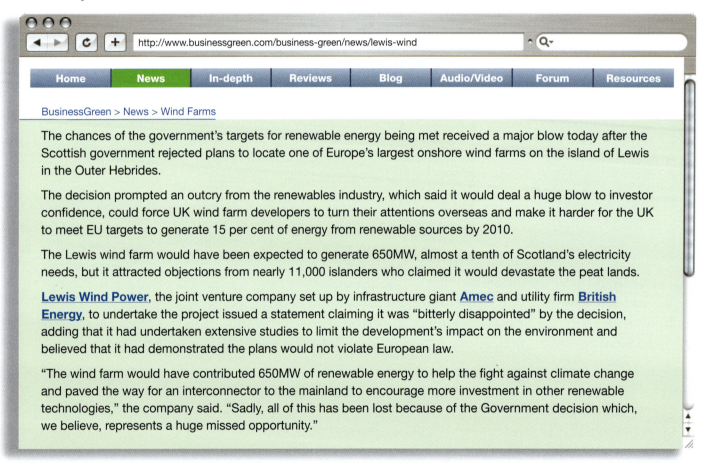

BusinessGreen > News > Wind Farms

The chances of the government's targets for renewable energy being met received a major blow today after the Scottish government rejected plans to locate one of Europe's largest onshore wind farms on the island of Lewis in the Outer Hebrides.

The decision prompted an outcry from the renewables industry, which said it would deal a huge blow to investor confidence, could force UK wind farm developers to turn their attentions overseas and make it harder for the UK to meet EU targets to generate 15 per cent of energy from renewable sources by 2010.

The Lewis wind farm would have been expected to generate 650MW, almost a tenth of Scotland's electricity needs, but it attracted objections from nearly 11,000 islanders who claimed it would devastate the peat lands.

Lewis Wind Power, the joint venture company set up by infrastructure giant **Amec** and utility firm **British Energy**, to undertake the project issued a statement claiming it was "bitterly disappointed" by the decision, adding that it had undertaken extensive studies to limit the development's impact on the environment and believed that it had demonstrated the plans would not violate European law.

"The wind farm would have contributed 650MW of renewable energy to help the fight against climate change and paved the way for an interconnector to the mainland to encourage more investment in other renewable technologies," the company said. "Sadly, all of this has been lost because of the Government decision which, we believe, represents a huge missed opportunity."

2 What advantages does the article state this wind farm would have brought? List as many as you can.

3 Why was the wind farm rejected according to the article?

4 'Islanders who claimed it would devastate the peat lands.' Why do you think the writer uses the word 'claimed' rather than 'said' or 'showed'?

5 The article uses the expression 'major blow' in the first paragraph to emphasise the seriousness of the situation. Write down a similar expression in the last paragraph which also seeks to emphasise this point to the reader.

6 After reading this article, do you agree or disagree that the government made the right decision in turning down the wind farm proposal? Explain your answer.

Activity 2

1 Now read the following article from the RSPB on the Lewis wind farm, written before the government made its decision.

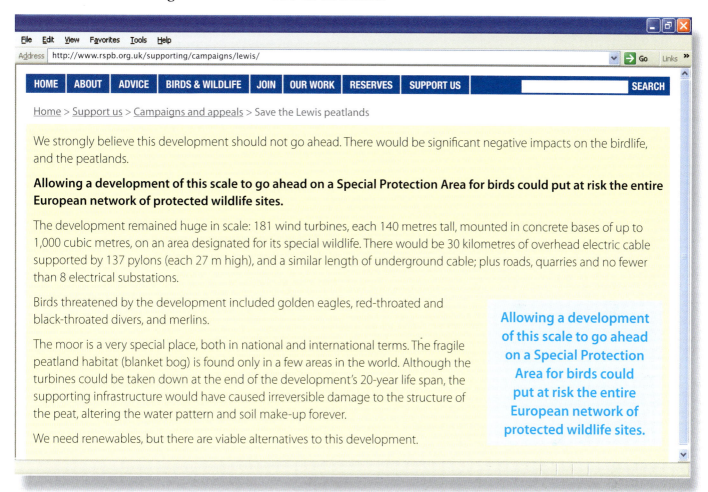

2 This article puts forward another reason for rejecting the wind farm that was not mentioned in the BusinessGreen.com article. What is it?

3 It is not obvious to everyone that peatlands are important. How does the RSPB article seek to persuade its readers that the peatlands must be protected?

4 The RSPB article uses the words 'fragile' and 'irreversible'. For each, explain what it means and explain what effect it is intended to have on the reader.

Self-evaluation

You have been identifying biased language to express a point of view and influence the reader. Use the table below to assess how well you are doing.

Beginner	Competent	Expert
I can comment on a writer's use of biased language and its effect on the reader	I can comment in detail on a writer's choice of biased language and how it contributes to the effect of the text	I can analyse how a writer's use of biased language manipulates the reader's response

Activity 3

In the previous two articles, the writers chose to emphasise some points about the proposed wind farm in Lewis and not others.

1 Complete the following table looking at which points were made by which article.

Point	Mentioned by BusinessGreen.com (yes/no)	Mentioned by RSPB (yes/no)
Birds will be seriously affected by the wind farm.		
We need to use more renewable energy.		
The wind farm would generate 10% of Scotland's electricity needs.		
The peatlands will be affected		
The peatlands are valuable and important and could be permanently damaged.		

2 Which two points can be found in both articles?

3 What does the RSPB think are the most important points about the Lewis wind farm?

4 What does BusinessGreen.com think are the most important points about the Lewis wind farm?

Activity 4

1 Read the passage below about nuclear power stations from the Scottish Government website, and answer the questions that follow.

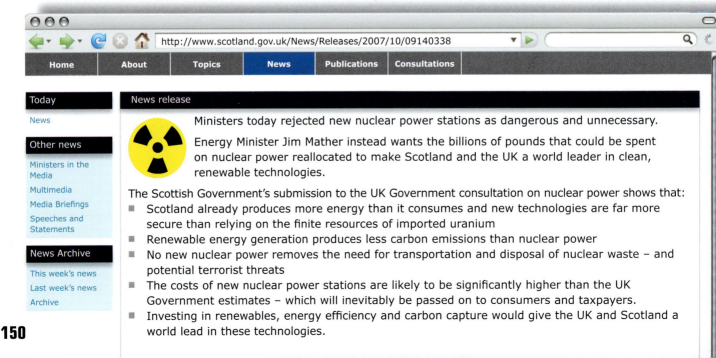

http://www.scotland.gov.uk/News/Releases/2007/10/09140338

Home   About   Topics   **News**   Publications   Consultations

Today
News

Other news
Ministers in the Media
Multimedia
Media Briefings
Speeches and Statements

News Archive
This week's news
Last week's news
Archive

News release

Ministers today rejected new nuclear power stations as dangerous and unnecessary.

Energy Minister Jim Mather instead wants the billions of pounds that could be spent on nuclear power reallocated to make Scotland and the UK a world leader in clean, renewable technologies.

The Scottish Government's submission to the UK Government consultation on nuclear power shows that:
- Scotland already produces more energy than it consumes and new technologies are far more secure than relying on the finite resources of imported uranium
- Renewable energy generation produces less carbon emissions than nuclear power
- No new nuclear power removes the need for transportation and disposal of nuclear waste – and potential terrorist threats
- The costs of new nuclear power stations are likely to be significantly higher than the UK Government estimates – which will inevitably be passed on to consumers and taxpayers.
- Investing in renewables, energy efficiency and carbon capture would give the UK and Scotland a world lead in these technologies.

2 Nuclear power stations need uranium in order to generate nuclear energy. Explain in your own words what is meant by 'new technologies are far more secure than relying on the finite resources of imported uranium'.

3 Why would building nuclear power stations and wind farms create carbon emissions? (Clue: think about what they are made of.)

Activity 5

1 Read the following passage from a newspaper article and answer the questions that follow.

'Scotland requires about 5.5 to 6 gigawatts of electricity to keep its offices running, its homes warm and its factories working,' Jim McDonald, director of Strathclyde University's centre of energy and environment points out. 'We can now generate almost 10 gigawatts and export the excess to England. With no replacements for Hunterston and Torness, that will stop. Nuclear power now provides 40 per cent of our power baseload. Without it, we would end up importing power and I don't see how a country seeking full autonomy can justify that.'

Indeed, if the rest of Britain decides, as expected, to replace its ageing atom plants with new ones – unlike Scotland – much of the electricity pumped north to fill the nation's power vacuum would be nuclear. Morally and economically, Scotland would be on dodgy ground.

So are our leaders really sure we can make it as an industrial power without nuclear energy? Can we definitely rely only on renewables to ensure our industrial strength? A brief glance at the options is illuminating. Our hydro-electric power capacity is near its limit, while wave and tidal energy technology, although of considerable promise, is in its infancy. That leaves us with wind, a source of immense potential but, like nuclear, bedevilled by committed opposition.

From *The Observer*,
Sunday 23rd September 2007

2 The last paragraph includes two questions. What effect are these questions intended to have on the reader?

3 Jim McDonald states nuclear energy provides 40% of the energy generated in Scotland. Look at the other figures he provides and work out how many gigawatts of energy are provided by non-nuclear sources.

4 Does your answer to the question above fit with McDonald's assertion that Scotland would have to import energy if it did not have nuclear power stations? Explain your answer.

5 'Wave and tidal energy technology, although of considerable promise, is in its infancy.' Explain this argument in your own words.

6 'Can we definitely rely only on renewables to ensure our industrial strength?' What is the Scottish Government's reply to that question? What is the writer of the article's reply to that question? Which do you find more convincing and why?

Writing Activity

Discursive writing

Is renewable energy the best way to prevent climate change?

Write an essay that gives your opinion on the question above. Use the articles on pages 148–151 to give you information and ideas. You should also think about additional information you might need to answer this question and research it on the internet.

You have three possible answers:

1 It is the best way to prevent to climate change.
2 It is not the best way to prevent climate change.
3 It is part/only part of the best way to prevent climate change.

You should consider the following points before writing your essay:

- Renewables are safe to use and will last forever.
- Renewables generate no carbon dioxide which is the major contributor to climate change.
- A lot of the technology for renewables is still at an early stage.
- Wind farms can destroy wildlife habitats.
- Many people object to living beside wind farms.
- Wind and solar power are not always available (the sun does not always shine and the wind does not always blow).
- Nuclear power does not cause global warming and has been used successfully for years.

Think of specific questions you would like to know the answer to **before** doing any internet research. Then look for the answers. For example:

Is nuclear power safe and effective?

Do wind farms always destroy wildlife?

Is wind power unreliable in Scotland or is there enough wind for reliable power generation?

Are there any other alternatives (carbon capture from conventional fossil fuel power stations)?

Remember what you have learned about writing in a persuasive way.

a   Make it clear at the beginning of the essay what you are going to be arguing. Your introduction should set out what you think the answer to this question is.

b   The topic sentence normally begins a paragraph and states the point that you will go on to develop in the rest of the paragraph.

c   Use well researched statistics, saying where you got them from. Relate them to something your readers can understand.

d   Try to use rhetorical questions, emotive language and other persuasive techniques to win the reader over to your side.

e   Bring in counter-arguments but remember to show why they should not persuade the reader – by showing that it is a weak argument or not as good as the arguments on the other side.

You will be assessed on the following criteria:

● your ability to present a sound argument with a clear line of thought, and relevant supporting evidence

● your ability to use information in this unit and from elsewhere, acknowledging your sources appropriately

● your ability to influence your reader through use of language, style and tone

● your spelling, punctuation and paragraphing should be accurate and your sentence structure should be appropriate.

7 Debating skills – rebuttal

You are learning:
● how to identify and rebut arguments.

An important skill in debating is to recognise arguments and counter them. Countering them is known as **rebuttal**. This is a test of your ability to listen to arguments and respond to what has just been said.

Activity 1

Look at the following argument about nuclear power. Three students have attempted to rebut the argument. Which rebuttal is best and why?

Argument: Nuclear power will prevent global warming as it does not generate carbon dioxide.

Rebuttal 1: I disagree. Nuclear power leaves radioactive waste, which is very dangerous.

Rebuttal 2: I disagree. Nuclear power cannot be used to power cars or heat homes, so we will still have to burn fossil fuels, which causes global warming.

Rebuttal 3: I disagree. Solar energy is the way forward.

Activity 2

Look at the following arguments about nuclear and renewable power. In pairs, decide which arguments best rebut each other.

1. The world will soon run out of gas, oil and eventually coal. Nuclear power is needed to replace these.

2. Nuclear power needs supplies of uranium and the world will run out of uranium too.

3. The wind does not blow all the time and the sun does not shine all the time. Therefore, renewable energy is not as reliable as nuclear energy.

4. If there is an accident at a nuclear power station, it could cause many deaths and contaminate land for thousands of years.

5. We can manage the risks associated with nuclear power. We cannot manage the risks associated with global warming, such as rising sea levels and mass starvation.

6. The world will always have supplies of sunshine, wind and tides to provide energy.

7. Nuclear power stations can only be used to provide electricity. You cannot have a car powered by nuclear fission.

8. Nuclear power stations have been generating power successfully and safely for years. Renewable energy technologies are not developed enough to meet all our energy needs.

Activity 3

1 In four groups, draw up a list of facts and arguments
   on the following topics:
   a advantages of nuclear energy
   b disadvantages of nuclear energy
   c advantages of renewable energy (find out about different
       kinds: solar, wind, hydro, tidal)
   d disadvantages of renewable energy (find out about different
       kinds: solar, wind, hydro, tidal)

2 Regroup into groups of four. Each group must include someone
   who has researched one of a–d in the first task for this activity.
   Each person has two minutes to explain their research to the
   rest of the group before playing 'The Rebuttal Game'.

3 Now play 'The Rebuttal Game':

   > One person begins by putting forward an argument about renewable or nuclear energy.

   > The next person has to reply, 'I totally disagree' and then give a reason to counter that argument.

   > That person must then make a point of their own.

   > The next person then has to disagree with the second person's argument and make their point, and so on.

   Remember: you do not have to make a point from your
   own research – you are free to use what you learned at the
   start of this activity from other members of the group.

Peer-evaluation

Which member of your group came up with the best rebuttal? Copy and
complete the following report and be prepared to share it with the class.

In my group the person who came up with the best rebuttal was:
The point he or she was rebutting was:
His/Her argument was:
This was an effective rebuttal because:

8 Debating skills – speechwriting

You are learning:
● how to structure a short speech effectively.

Writing a speech is different from writing an essay. If a reader is confused or misses something in an essay, he or she can read it again. If a listener is confused or misses something in a speech, there is no going back. It is therefore important for a speech to be clearly structured and to include techniques such as repetition to help the listener remember the key points.

Activity 1

1   Look at this useful formula for writing a five minute speech.

Introduction: set out your argument and briefly state three points you will be making in support of your speech. (1 minute)

Point 1: Explain your first point. Give evidence to support it and explain why this evidence backs up your point. (1 minute)

Repeat for points 2 and 3. (1 minute each)

Conclusion: Remind the audience of the three points you made and why they are convincing. (1 minute)

2   Look at the following introductions to speeches, saying them aloud if possible. In pairs, decide which is the most effective and why.

① 'Imagine Edinburgh, empty and abandoned, apart from a few rats with enormous tumours. Imagine North Berwick's beaches closed because of radioactive particles. Imagine most of the Lothians unusable for farming as the soil is contaminated. And imagine over a million Scots dying of cancer.

One human error at Torness nuclear power station could cause all that.'

② 'I am going to explain why I believe that nuclear power is the best way to prevent global warming. First I will explain why nuclear energy provides clean, effective, carbon neutral power. Then I will go on to explain why the technology is safe and how it has been used in this country and elsewhere to generate power with success. Finally I will explain why nuclear power is far better than any alternative energy available today.'

③ 'Many people have strong feelings about nuclear energy. Some people think it is dangerous and are worried about nuclear waste. Other people say it has been used safely for years. I am going to give you some facts and figures about nuclear power before giving my opinion about it.'

3   In pairs, look at the following conclusions to speeches and decide which is most effective and why.

①

Renewable energy is safe and with more investment could be cheap and effective as well. With many people throughout the world facing starvation because of global warming, with sea levels rising and oil fast running out, can we really afford not to invest in it?

②

In my opinion, renewable energy would be a good idea, because it does not pollute and there is no danger of us running out of the world's resources of sunshine or wind. On the other hand, it does have some drawbacks because it is not always sunny and the wind does not blow all the time. Other people may have different opinions.

③

In my speech I have shown that we have to have renewable energy. We cannot keep burning fossil fuels and causing global warming. I have shown that renewable energy is safe and does not pollute the environment. I have also shown that there is a wide variety of options available, some tried and tested and some of which need more investment.

Activity 2

Consider these possible features of a conclusion. Which features do you think are most useful and which are least useful? Write a paragraph explaining your choice.

- a balanced statement looking at both sides
- a clear line of thought
- alliteration to make it more memorable and interesting for your audience
- a question to get your audience thinking
- a joke to get your audience laughing
- repetition to help the audience remember points better

Knowledge about language Rhetorical questions

Not every question is a rhetorical question. 'Can we really afford not to invest in it?' is a rhetorical question as it pushes the listener or reader towards the answer 'no'. A more neutral question is: 'Should we build more nuclear power stations?' There is nothing in this question to push the reader in one direction rather than another.

1   For each of the following questions say whether they are rhetorical or not rhetorical and explain why.

- Is wind energy the way forward?
- Can we really say with any certainty that nuclear power stations do not pose any threat to the people who live near them?
- Is 'Big Brother' an enjoyable programme?
- Are school dinners always healthy?
- Should we allow a system of taxation where the poor pay more tax than the rich?

2   Write some rhetorical questions of your own.

Talking and Listening Activity

Collaborative presentations

In this unit, you have read a range of texts around the themes of renewable energy and nuclear energy, including arguments for and against both.

Your task

You will give a group presentation on one aspect of the renewable/nuclear energy debate.

Return to the four groups that were used for research in Activity 3 on page 155:

a advantages of nuclear energy

b disadvantages of nuclear energy

c advantages of renewable energy (find out about different kinds: solar, wind, hydro, tidal)

d disadvantages of renewable energy (find out about different kinds: solar, wind, hydro, tidal)

Each group needs to contain up to five members. Each member is responsible for one minute of the presentation. Your presentation should include:

- an introduction
- a minute to introduce and develop the first point
- a minute to introduce and develop the second point
- a minute to introduce and develop the third point
- a conclusion.

If there are only four members then one person should do both the introduction and conclusion.

Stage 1:
Together the group must decide on the three main points of the presentation. The person doing the introduction and the person doing the conclusion must both know what all the points are so they can summarise them in their sections.

Stage 2:
Individually each member of the group must prepare the part of the presentation for which they are responsible. Make your points clear and memorable, through using language features such as alliteration, repetition and questions.

Stage 3:
The group must then put the presentation together and check the following:

- are there three clear and distinctive points to the argument
- does the introduction reflect what will come in the main part of the speech
- does the conclusion effectively sum up the case made?

Review each other's work. Look for alliteration, questions and repetition used effectively. Make sure you link the different parts of the presentation.

You will be assessed on:

- your ability to work well as a member of a group
- the clarity and persuasiveness of your part of the presentation
- your ability to understand and engage with a presentation on an issue that another group has covered.

	Talking – Presenting	Listening – Understanding, analysing and evaluating
Beginner	I can use appropriate vocabulary and explain my point clearly.	I can show my understanding of a presentation by commenting, with evidence, on the points raised.
Competent	I can use appropriate vocabulary, register and explain my ideas fully and clearly.	I can explain what points were made in the presentation and explain why I agree or disagree with them.
Expert	I can use suitable vocabulary to communicate effectively to my audience. I can support my ideas with relevant detail.	I can give detailed evaluative comments, supported by evidence, on the presentation I have heard.

You can use these criteria to make peer and self-assessments as you practise your presentation and watch other groups.

Active listening

When you are listening your mind should be fully engaged, thinking about the points you are hearing and deciding whether you agree or disagree. Are there any weaknesses in the argument? What evidence does the speaker put forward to support his or her points and does that evidence really prove what the speaker is trying to prove?

It often helps to take notes – but be selective. Don't try to write down everything the speaker says – you won't be able to keep up with what is being said.

Listen to another group's presentation. Then write a brief evaluation covering the questions that follow.

1 What three points did the group make in order to support their argument?

2 Choose **either** a point you found convincing and explain why you found it convincing **or** a point you found unconvincing and explain why you found it unconvincing.

   Remember that when you are explaining why something was convincing or unconvincing, you are not just discussing the point itself, but whether the speaker presented it effectively and memorably and supported it with convincing evidence.

3 Give the group 'two stars and a wish': congratulate them on two things they did well and give them one thing to improve for next time. Be specific.

Heinemann is an imprint of Pearson Education Limited, a company incorporated in England and Wales, having its registered office at Edinburgh Gate, Harlow, Essex, CM20 2JE. Registered company number: 872828

www.heinemann.co.uk

Heinemann is the registered trademark of Pearson Education Limited

Unit 1 versioned from original material by Esther Menon.
Units 2 and 6 versioned from original material by David Grant.
Unit 3 versioned from original material by Julia Hubbard.
Unit 4 versioned from original material by Richard Durant.
Unit 5 versioned from original material by Sam Custance.

Text © Pearson Education Limited 2009

First published 2009

13

10 9 8 7 6

British Library Cataloguing in Publication Data is available from the British Library on request.

ISBN 978 0 435 22503 2

Designed and produced by Kamae Design, Oxford
Original illustrations © Pearson Education Limited, 2009
Illustrated by Paul McCaffrey, Tony Forbes, Jo Taylor, Paco Cavero, Kathryn Baker, Majorie Dumortier
Cover design by Pete Stratton
Picture research by Elena Wright
Printed and bound in China (CTPS/06)

Acknowledgements

The authors and publisher would like to thank the following for permission to reproduce photographs:

Unit 1: p5 (mobile phone) iStockphoto; pp5, 6 (boy on computer) iStockphoto; p5 (teenagers checking text message) iStockphoto; p6 (Blackberry) Rex Features/ Mark Obstfeld; p10 Alamy Images/eye-D Prod; p14 Time & Life Pictures/Getty Images; p16 Corbis/Daniel Dal Zennaro/EPA; p22 Danny Lawson/PA Archive/PA Photos; p23 (top) pumpkin pictures/Alamy; p23 (bottom) WoodyStock/Alamy; p24 (left) PhotoDisc; p24 (right) Corbis; p25 Pearson Education Ltd/Steve Shott 2006; p27 Cornstock Images. **Unit 2:** p34 Shutterstock/Galyna Andrushko; p38 Viorika/iStockphoto; p56 Corbis/ Tim McGuire. **Unit 3:** pp57, 58 (Argyll coastline) David Robertson/Alamy; p58 (Tokyo) Photolibrary; p58 (Menara Dayabumi) Alamy Images/Laurie Strachan; p58 (sunrise) iStockphoto; p60 (top, middle and bottom) iStockphoto; p64 (top) Corbis/Bob Krist; p64 (bottom) Still Pictures/Chlaus Lotscher; p67 Corbis/Gary Braasch; p68 Ariadne Van Zandbergen/Africanpictures/Majority World; p71 (top) Getty Images; p71 (bottom) Mark Dean/Alamy; p72 (top) Mary Evans Picture Library; p72 (bottom) Corbis/Francesc Muntada; p74 LOOK Die Bildagentur der Fotografen GmbH/Alamy; p76 Andrzej Stajer/ iStockPhoto; p77 David Keaton/CORBIS; p78 Blackbeck/iStockphoto; p81 TENGKU BAHAR/AFP/Getty Images. **Unit 4:** p83 (top left) Corbis/Hulton-Deutsch Collection; p83 (top right) Getty Images/William Vanderson/Fox Photos; p83 (bottom), 93, 104 Topham Picturepoint; p84 Rex Features/Nils Jorgensen; p86 (H G Wells) Mary Evans Picture Library/Alamy; pp86, 87 Kobal; p88 School Library Association/Kathy Lemaire; p89 Corbis; p90 Bettmann/CORBIS; p91 Roger Tidman/CORBIS; p93 (top) Scottish Photo Library; p94 (Poster A) Corbis/Stapleton Collection; p94 (Poster B) The Art Archive/ Eileen Tweedy; p94 (bottom) Alamy Images/Lebrecht Music and Arts Photo Library; p96 Rex Features/Nick Rogers; p98 Corbis/Jon Hicks; p101 Corbis/Bettmann; p102 Topham Picturepoint; p106 Sipa Press/Rex Features. **Unit 5:** pp109 (top left), 112 Rex Features/Alastair Muir; pp109 (top right), 120 Topham Picturepoint/Universal Pictorial Press Photo; p120 (left) Capital Pictures; p120 (top right) ITV/Rex Features; p120 (middle right) Rex Features/NCUPHOTOBANK; p122 Rex Features/C.S Goldwyn/ Everett; p124 Kobal Collection/Lake Film; p126 Kobal Collection/Lake Film; p132 Alastair Muir/ Alamy. **Unit 6:** p135 (top) Rex Features/ITV; p135 (middle), 142 Rex Features/Jonathan Hordle; pp135 (bottom), 139 Corbis/Toby Melville/Reuters; p138 Pearson Education Ltd/Photodisc; p140 NICHOLAS ROBERTS/AFP/Getty Images; p142 (Big Brother logo) Rex Features; p142 (bottom right) Rex Features/Jonathan Hordle; p143 Getty Images/ Chris Weeks; p144 (left) Rex Features/ITV; p144 (middle left) Kobal Collection/NBC TV; p144 (right) Photoshot/UPPA; p152 SIMON FRASER/SCIENCE PHOTO LIBRARY; p155 Macduff Everton/Getty Images.

Every effort has been made to contact copyright holders of material reproduced in this book. Any omissions will be rectified in subsequent printings if notice is given to the publishers.

'The Big Spring Clean' used with permission of Ski Club of Great Britain and Facebook; Extract from Young Scot website used with the kind permission of Young Scot – The National Youth Information Agency for Scotland; 'How far would you go?' by Sophie Radice. Copyright Guardian News & Media Ltd 2007. Used with permission; Moby diary extract used by permission of Kelly Money; Joan Lennon 'Blogspot' used with kind permission of Joan Lennon; Book cover from Wow! 366 used with permission of Scholastic; Diary extract from James Boswell; Extract from Logotron used with the kind permission of Logotron Limited; NASA images used with permission; Extract from Virtual Festivals used with permission www.virtualfestivals.com; Article 'How TV is (quite literally) killing us' from Remotely Controlled by Dr. Aric Sigman, published by Vermilion. Reprinted by permission of The Random House Group Ltd; Brautigan, Richard: 'A Scarlatti Tilt' from REVENGE OF THE LAWN. Copyright © 1971 by Richard Brautigan. Used by permission of the Author's estate; Extract from 'Death and the Boy'. Reprinted by permission of United Agents Limited on behalf of Anthony Horowitz © 2007; Extract from 'At the Edge of the Country' by Alexander McCall Smith. From In Shorts 3 – The Macallan Scotland on Sunday Short Story Collection, published by Polygon. Used by permission of David Higham Associates; Extract from 'Killer Mum' by Janet Paisley. © Janet Paisley. From the book Shouting it Out published by Hodder & Stoughton, 1995, edited by Tom Pow; Extract from 'Hurricane Jack' by Neil Munro; Extract from 'Silver Linings' by Joan Lingerd, from The Wild Ride and Other Scottish Stories, published by Puffin. Used by permission of David Higham Associates; Extract from 'Mary Moon and the Stars' by Janice Galloway. Used by permission of AP Watt Ltd on behalf of Janice Galloway; Extract from 'A Time to Dance' Copyright © Bernard MacLaverty. Reproduced by permission of the author c/o Rogers, Coleridge & White Ltd., 20 Powis Mews, London W11 1JN; Extract from 'She' by Rosa Guy from the RHCB edition of Sixteen: Short Stories by Gallo. Used with permission of Random House. Extract from 'The Cure' © Liz Lochhead. Used by permission of the Rod Hall Agency; Extract from 'Sharlo's Strange Bargain' © Ralph Prince. Used with kind permission of the author's estate; Extracts from 'Kreativ Riting' © Brian McCabe, used with kind permission of the author; Extract from 'Leaving Assynt' © Anne MacLeod. Used by permission of author via Jenny Brown Associates; Short story 'Saskatchewan' © Lorn Macintyre. Used by permission of Argyll Publishing; Short story 'All that Glisters' From Hieroglyphics and Other Stories by Anne Donovan, first published in Great Britain by Canongate Books Ltd, 14 High Street, Edinburgh, EH1 1TE; Front cover of ROUGH GUIDE TO PERU 6th Edition by Dilwyn Jenkins (Rough Guides, 1997, 2006). Copyright © Dilwyn Jenkins 1992, 1997, 2006. Used with permission of Penguin Books; Cover from DVD of 'Around the World in 80 Days' used by permission of The Random House Group Ltd; Contents pages from ROUGH GUIDE TO ICELAND 3rd edition (Rough Guides 2001, 2004, 2007). Text copyright © David Leffman and James Proctor 2001, 2004, 2007. Used with permission of Penguin Books; Extract and map from Insight Pocket Guide to the Seychelles. Reprinted with permission of Insight Guides; Extracts from 'The Runaway Bride' by Catherine Jones. Used by kind permission of Talesmag; Extract from 'Living in Ghana' by Magdalena Travis. Used by kind permission of Talesmag; 'Summer in Skye' by Alexander Smith; Diary Extract by Lady Florence Dixie; Extract from Argentina by Florian von der Vecht; Article 'Instant Weekend' by Chris West as appeared in the Sunday Times, 23/09/2007. Used by permission of NI Syndication; Extract from Mountains of the Mind by Robert Macfarlane. Used by permission of Granta Publications; City of God by St. Augustine; Quote by Bill Bryson used with the kind permission of the author; Extract from Tourism Concern used with kind permission from Tourism Concern – ww.tourismconcern. org.uk; Extract about transatlantic flights © UN Atlas of the Oceans, www.oceansatlas. org; Extract about Scottish tourism used with kind permission of the Scottish Parliament; 'Celebrate Scotland' poster. Used with kind permission of Visit Scotland www. visitscotland.com; Extract from Strange Meeting by Susan Hill, published by Penguin, Copyright © Susan Hill, 1971, 1989. Reproduced by permission of Sheil Land Associates Ltd; Extract from 'War of the Worlds' by HG Wells. Used by permission of A.P. Watt Ltd on behalf of The Literary Executors of the Estate of HG Wells; Extract and book cover from Remembrance by Theresa Breslin, published by Doubleday. Reprinted by permission of The Random House Group Ltd; 'Logan Braes' by Robert Burns; Poem 'In Memoriam' by Ewart Alen Mackintosh; Poem 'The Mither's Lament' by Sydney Goodsir Smith, from Collected poems 1941–1975, John Calder, 1975. Used by permission; Poem 'We Shall Remember Them' by Sheila Parry. Used with kind permission of Sheila Parry; Poem 'For a Dead African' by Dennis Brutus. Used by kind permission of the author; 'Outbreak of War' Speech. 22nd August–3rd September 1939. Ministry of Information: London: No. 1 (1939) Section V. 3rd September 1939. Broadcast by the Rt. Hon. Neville Chamberlain. M.P., Prime Minister. Material Source: University of Birmingham; 'We Shall Meet Them on the Beaches' speech © Winston S. Churchill. Reproduced with permission of Curtis Brown Ltd. London on behalf of The Estate of Winston Churchill; 'Blood, Toil, Tears and Sweat' speech © Winston S. Churchill. Reproduced with permission of Curtis Brown Ltd. London on behalf of The Estate of Winston Churchill; Speech 'A stand for peace, not a rush for war', Crown Copyright. Extract and book cover from Hieroglyphics and Other Stories by Anne Donovan, first published in Great Britain by Canongate Books Ltd, 14 High Street, Edinburgh, EH1 1TE; 'Hieroglyphics' playscript from Scottish Plays for Schools published by Hodder Gibson. Used by permission of the author; Use of extract from transcript of Only Fools and Horses Christmas Special by John Sullivan. Reprinted with the kind permission of John Sullivan; Extract from 'Gregory's Girl' © Bill Forsyth. Used by permission of Cambridge University Press; Extract from 'My makeup turned me into a monster' from no. 698 17-30 April 2008. Reprinted by permission of Panini UK Ltd; 'Vicky B does Casual' Fri. June 13, 2008. Used by permission of Closer Online. closeronline.co.uk; Article 'We shouldn't take pleasure in the plight of Lehman Brothers' employees' by Tracy Corrigan, The Daily Telegraph, 16/09/08. Used by permission; Extract from the Daily Record used with kind permission of the Daily Record; 'Now we all have to pay for the bank's mistakes' by Richard Ingrams. © The Independent, Saturday, 20th September, 2008. Used with permission of The Independent; 'A curse on cruelty TV' from the Daily Mail. Used by permission of Solo Syndication; 'Lewis Wind Farm Rejection' used with the kind permission of BusinessGreen; 'Save the Lewis Peatlands' extract from the RSPB website used with permission from the RSPB; 'Ministers say no to nuclear power' © The Scottish Government. Used with permission; 'Why we need our own nuclear power:' by Robin McKie.Copyright Guardian News & Media Ltd 2007. Used with permission.